GW01564411

AN OLD FASHIONE.
SIMPLE, TRIED A

To Patricia
Card Shop near Todo Todo.
July 16th 2005
To ME Love ME

To MARIA

ENJOY YOUR COOKING
Love from
Pat & Milly xx

An Old Fashioned Cook Book:
Simple, Tried and Tested

Lynn Williams

The Pentland Press Limited
Edinburgh · Cambridge · Durham · USA

First published in 2000 by
The Pentland Press Ltd.
I Hutton Close
South Church
Bishop Auckland
Durham

British Library Cataloguing in Publication Data.
A catalogue record for this book is available
from the British Library.

ISBN 1 85821 730 X

Typeset by George Wishart & Associates, Whitley Bay.
Printed and bound by Lintons Printers, Co. Durham.

*To my devoted husband,
with love and thanks.*

Contents

Cold Sweets

Biscuits and Cookies

Icing for Cakes

Flavourings for Butter Cream Icing

Salads

Salad Dressing

Sandwich Fillings

Sauces, Stuffings, and Miscellaneous

········· · · · · · · · · · ·
Author's Note
········· · · · · · · · · · ·

FROM THE YEAR 1910

When old people get together, invariably they talk about the 'Good old days'.
They start remembering...

Now that I have time to recall some of the everyday happenings of my past life, I can remember them quite vividly, as if it had all happened yesterday.

My father's family had emigrated to America a few years earlier and suggested that my father should bring his wife and young son over there, where they could have a better life, knowing that times were pretty hard at that time in England. They offered to pay all expenses, but my mother was unwilling. She hated the sea, and the thought of a long sea voyage. My father did all in his powers to persuade her, but to no avail. Then when she knew she was pregnant with me, that settled the matter, I was to be born in England.

Incidentally, years later, when my father died, I resumed the correspondence which he had with my cousin 'Will' in America, and eventually my daughter and I travelled to America.

I found it very interesting to read some of my late father's letters, which had been kept in a library, as they were thought to be a true representation of everyday living in England during the years 1914 to 1958.

One of my earliest recollections was of seeing my grandmother, who had come all the way from America to visit her son and family. She was holding her outstretched arms to me and saying 'Come along darling, walk to me'. She did teach me to walk, I can clearly remember the last quick rush into her arms.

Years afterwards, when I recalled the incident to my mother, she said 'Impossible, you were only a baby,' but was aghast when I actually described what my grandmother was wearing, and how she looked.

Now, even all these years later, I can still picture that scene, so clearly. My memory of my first day at school, on my fifth birthday, my mother had made me two gingham overalls, one a pink check and the other a blue one. So I was wearing the pink check overall over my best dress, and taken to school by my mother. She held my hand as we went to see the Headmistress in her tiny office. As they were busy talking I was fascinated by four pictures side by side on the walls all about the little pigs being taken to market, and I really could understand what they were doing.

That same afternoon I was given a wooden box with a sliding lid and on opening it I found a mass of tangled wool of many colours and was told to separate the wool into strands of each colour, red with red, blue with blue etc. While I was doing this I distinctly remember thinking, why did it all get entangled in such a state. However, I soon forgot this nonsense when I was given a slate and a slate pencil, and told to draw. I did not mind going to school, except that my brother five years my senior was in charge, but he resented having to take a girl to school when he wanted to be with his 'pals', so I was invariably left to find my own way there, with strict instructions not to tell Mam or else . . .

I soon learned to be independent, and joined in with other children in the school playground for games of skipping, ring-a-roses and hopscotch, then later learning to play with tops and whips and bowling hoops. As we all got a little older we understood that school was not to be all fun and games, we had to learn more serious things.

I had been rather a sickly child, always seemed to have a childish ailment, bronchitis, whooping cough, measles, chicken pox, heavy colds. I recall my mother asking the Doctor 'will she get over it'? What 'it' was, I did not understand, but his answer was 'she will be as fit as a fiddle after she is seven'. Well, not long after this, I developed scarlet fever and was taken to hospital, and was there for six weeks. During my stay there, one particular night we were all awakened by very bright lights and noise. The children who were well enough stood up in their beds looking out of the ward windows and up at the sky. I was one of them, watching the German Zeppelin in flames, fortunately missing us on its way down. To us children it was very exciting, we did not realize the horror of the flames and the deaths of the people inside. But of course it was exciting to the adults, because they saw the enemy in flames.

A week later I was well again. I left hospital with straight hair and a shrunken winter coat. I had lost my curls and my coat had lost its smart new look, we had both been well and truly doused with a very strong antiseptic.

Not long after this episode there was great excitement again. The War was over!! It was the day of the Armistice. The children were given flags, my mother told me to hold on tight to mine because it cost 4 pence, and to keep on waving. It was not much fun really, because the noise was awful and I became tired of waving, but I cheered up a bit when I remembered about the big kitchen knife, a gully my mother called it. Each time she opened the cutlery drawer in the kitchen table she would lift up the gully and say 'If the German comes here he will get this,' and she would screw up her mouth and I knew she meant that she would do something awful. But now everything was alright. The German would not come.

The next few years of my life were quite unremarkable, my mother was proud of her little home and cleaned until everything sparkled. We lived in a street. We were lucky; we had the only house to have a 'proper' lavatory, my mother harassed the landlord so much. I think he was pleased to install one for peace sake, but it was a great asset, even though it was down the yard. The only water tap was there too, next to the wash house, which made things easier on wash days.

My father worked very hard as a blast furnaceman. He used to work shifts, which meant mornings 6a.m. to 2p.m. or 2p.m.to 10p.m. or nights 10p.m. to 6a.m., with an occasional day or weekend off. He had to walk to and from work, about two miles. I used to take his meals sometimes at weekends, when he worked what he called his long shift. Mother used to put his dinner in a basin, wrap it tight with a cloth, fill a can with tea, and I was told to hurry with it to my father. When I reached his place of work, I saw my Dad almost bent double, pulling the huge iron barrow. He looked so sad and tired. When he saw me he would straighten up and say 'Hello Honey,' and dump the barrow and come and cuddle me, then we went into the hut and we would sit together and chat for a while as he enjoyed his meal, after he would thank and kiss me and give me a silver three-penny piece. I would trot back home, loving my Dad, thinking he should not be working as hard as that. I did not realize at that time, but he had been lucky to be even working, because the dole years were soon on us and things became really bad, very few men had jobs and those who had, had poor wages.

Fortunately, my mother was a good cook and a good manager. Each Friday she would empty her purse onto her lap and count out her money. So much for rent, coal, gas, ticket, food, milk etc; there was never much left over. She had a friend, a widow, who had two daughters who went to the same school as me. This lady also had a gentleman lodger, who she said was 'very good' to her. To eke out her existence she used to issue 'tickets', whereby one could get a one pound ticket, or book of coupons, to obtain a poundsworth of goods at specified shops, probably for clothing, shoes, etc, to pay off at a shilling a week for twenty weeks, plus a shilling extra for the book; no doubt she would also get something from the shop too. However, a friend she certainly was.

A year or so after my mother became friendly with her, the girls in our class at school sat for exams to enter secondary school. Quite a few of us passed. When my mother heard I had passed too, she told me 'not to get excited', as I should not be able to go, as we could not afford the uniform. I was, of course, very upset, as all my friends seemed to be going. Mother's friend called and proudly said both her girls were going too. She could not believe it when my mother told her my news.

She went home and thought about it. She possessed a Sunray skirt (a skirt of many pleats). In those days, pleats were not permanent, so she washed, pressed, and made this into a gym dress, then washed, ironed and altered one of the lodger's white shirts, and presented them the following week. Needless to say, I wept with joy. They fitted perfectly. 'Now,' she said, 'you only need your panama and badge and you will do for the summer term.'

I must have knocked on every door within a mile of our house to see if anyone wanted 'messages or jobs'. At last I made enough to buy a one shilling and eleven pence panama hat and badge at two shillings and sixpence. I do not think there was a prouder pair than my friend and I that day we started our new school, and even though my mother's friend is long gone, I cherish her memory. . .

My father did manage to get a job again, and was able to take things easier. He did the 'Limericks' and competitions in *John Bull* and *Titbits*, the weekly papers, and each week he won a book, or received a two shilling and sixpence voucher again. Pretty soon the bookcase filled up, and each Easter he would tell me he would buy me a new outfit, and sure enough he would manage to win enough to rig me out and buy something new for mother. The only snag, when he took me to buy shoes they were always too tight, more so the next day, Sunday, when he took me on our usual walk.

We went somewhere different every week, but always in the country. We both loved the river banks and hedgerows, and he used to teach me the names of the birds and wild flowers, in other words, he taught me to love wildlife.

I am sorry that children of today have missed the glory of bathing in streams, picking flowers and fruit in the country and watercress in the clear, clean streams . . .

But, now I was older, I had to come down to earth and learn in my new school. I learnt to listen when the pupils bragged about their holidays or what they brought in their sandwiches for lunch, and when fine weather, took my lunch in to the playground out of sight of the others. Although not hungry any more, we had to be frugal.

I went to help my grandmother on Saturdays. One of my mother's sisters had died, and left three young boys, so the boys and their Dad all went to live with my grandmother. Each Saturday at 8a.m. I was sent off to walk the three miles to her house, to do whatever jobs she had for me. I grumbled to myself sometimes, when she sent me straight back up the bank two miles to do some shopping, and to hurry back, because there was a lot of work to be done.

When I got back I had to start scrubbing the floors downstairs. She also had a big dog which was always in the way. When I finished downstairs I had to go upstairs and sweep and dust. I used to be worn out when I came down and had to give a hand at filling a bath for the boys in front of the fire. Having a brother, I soon got used to seeing boys in the bath.

In the summertime, after we had finished and had some tea, my grandma would say 'come on, we will go in the garden and see what there is.' The garden was quite big at the back of the house. She knew I was fond of flowers; even though she was kept busy she found time to grow her own vegetables and flowers. Her garden had a delightful mixture of the old fashioned flowers – mignonette, phlox, marguerites, scabious, candytuft, nemesia, gypsophila, pinks and paeonies.

I used to watch as she picked and I knew when she had finished, she used to tie them with strong grass and hand them to me, and before I said goodbye she would say 'now let me see', and put her hand under her apron for her purse which she would slowly open and take out a sixpence. I would hold out my hand and say 'No, grandma, you really should not,' hoping all the while that she would, then she would give me a quick kiss and say 'be off now.' Quite often I spent two pence of that on the tram fare home . . .

One Saturday before Christmas, when I went to do my usual chores at my grandmother's, I found everything in utter chaos. The place was a shambles in more ways than one, actually a shambles.

My grandmother had three sons living near, each sharing the expense and care of a pig, which was in a sty in grandmother's garden, where she also kept a few chickens.

At that time there was some law or other about pig keeping and killing. I am not sure why they did it, but the pig was killed, scraped and cleaned, and cut up, in one of my grandmother's bedrooms. So all the boiling water had to be taken up and down stairs. Finally, it was cut up into joints and given to various members of the family for Christmas. All this happened during the night, so suspicions were not aroused, and my job was to finish off what cleaning needed to be done after all that trampling up and down stairs Needless to say, I do still think of that. Sometimes, when I see a pork joint, was it worth it?? Certainly at that time it was, I'm sure . . .

I was 14 years old when I had my first 'follower'. I had just finished working at my grandmother's one Saturday, and having a cup of tea, when there was a knock at the door, my uncle opened it, and there was a young man from the next street, he said he had come to accompany me home. My uncle had a quick 'Comfab' with grandmother, who decided he was a good character, so being forewarned, he was allowed to escort me home. Well, I thought as we walked home, I do not know what all the fuss was about, because he was too old at 18 years at least, had nothing exciting to say, and I was very bored, and more annoyed, because we walked all the way to my home, while if I had been alone I could have ridden on a tram. As it happened, I did not go many more times after this, because my mother was ill and I was needed at home . . .

My mother, like most of the housewives at that time, kept to a routine plan of the work to be done each day of the week. Monday was always washday. Tuesday, usually ironing, general tidy up in the house. Wednesday, odd jobs, often visits from friends or to friends. Thursday, baking day. Friday, cleaning. Saturday, shopping. Sunday, free day. Monday, my mother would get up very early to light the fire under the copper which she filled with water. Then clothes were sorted out in piles, whites, coloureds, wools and delicates. Whites were dealt with first, put in a tub with warm water, and 'possed', with a wooden dolly, rinsed by hand, then put to boil afterwards, well rinsed, then 'Blued', with 'Reckitt's Dolly Blue', which made them look sparkling white, and starched if necessary. The heavy hand-turned mangle squeezed out most of the water. If the weather was good the clothes were hung outside to dry on a clothes line. Then followed the washing of the rest of the clothes and bedding. Sometimes in the winter the washing would be frozen stiff, so that they had to be dried overnight on the ceiling racks. Obviously, the ironing did not always get done until Tuesday. So while the irons, (the old flat irons) were heating up on the fire, my mother would prepare vegetables for a pan of broth, which would simmer slowly until half an hour or so before dinner time, when she would pop a few onion dumplings on top of the broth, covering the pan with the lid again. When we arrived in from school a lovely onion smell would greet us and we would realize how hungry we were.

The kitchen was a lovely homely place to be in, especially in the winter. My father had made an extra long toasting fork and he used to sit me on his knee while we took turns at holding the fork to make toast, which when brown he would spread with beef dripping, sprinkled with a little salt and pepper, and we would sit snugly munching, really enjoying ourselves. Occasionally, when it was my Dad's day off, he would buy some kippers or bloaters, and gave my mother some money to and enjoy herself at the 'Pictures' (she really loved to see films). Off she would go and Dad would get out the trivet (again something he made specially for grilling), and make up the fire, so it was red and glowing, without smoke, and then begin the ritual of cooking the fish. He would watch over them patiently, turning when necessary. Then when they were cooked to his satisfaction, the pair of us would have a feast. Afterwards, we would tidy up and make things shipshape again, but when my mother returned home, there were harsh words from her about the smell in the kitchen, and the fat splashes on her precious range, which she kept immaculate by black leading to a high polish. We listened and tried to look sorry, but we really were quite happy, we had enjoyed ourselves . . .

The day before baking day which was usually on a Thursday, the oven had to be cleaned out, which meant the top cavity of the oven, called the 'Flu' had to be cleared of soot with a special brush and rake, and all the cinders raked out from under the oven. So on baking day the fire was lit quite early and extra heat was obtained by pushing hot coals or wood under the oven. On the opposite side of the fireplace was a side tank which was filled each day with cold water, so when the fire was lit the water became hot and was ladled out when required for washing up, cleaning etc. At the same time a kettle was always kept filled on top of the tank, at the ready for tea-making. There was a trivet for pans to rest on and often a hanging hook for a kettle or pan. I used to like baking day. When I was very young my mother used to give me little jobs like stoning raisins, grating nutmeg or suet, but I was very careful not to grate my fingers. My treat was 'licking' the bowls after cake-making or being given a piece of pastry to make my own cake, all good experience for later life.

Occasionally, mother would buy herrings from the street hawker, at seven for sixpence, and she would clean and gut them and souse them in vinegar, and we would have rollmops for tea with water bread, fresh from the oven (see recipe). The heavy metal oven sheets, which were always warm, were very useful in the winter, when they would be wrapped in pieces of old blankets and used as bed warmers.

In those days, before modern cleaners, fridges and cooking appliances, it must have been very hard work with just the basic necessities in the kitchen.

Saturday was always very exciting for me when I was a child. In the afternoons, my brother and I would go to the Matinee, a film show for children at the local cinema. The children would all queue up at the doors, and when they opened there was a stampede, everyone rushing to get a seat, and when settled, would open up the packet of sweets. My brother and I were each given 4 pence every Saturday. 2 pence for the Matinee and 2 pence for sweets. We always chose the sweets that lasted a long time, my brother would choose black bullets and I chose pear drops. The film was usually a comic, and part of a serial like 'The Adventures of Pearl White', or the 'Clutching Hand', sometimes, to me quite terrifying, but we loved it all the same. After tea we all used to go to the market, my Dad would come too if he was not working. After 6 o'clock the butchers in the indoor market used to auction the leftovers of meat and eventually my mother would get a large joint of meat for about 2 shillings, and sometimes a few sausages thrown in with it for free. In the outdoor market, which in the winter was lit by acetylene flares, flowers, vegetables and fruit also were sold off cheaply. Clutching our purchases, and rather tired, occasionally mother suggested a treat, and we would go into one of the pie and pea tents, and have a 3 pence plate of peas and vinegar...

In later years the family used to celebrate New Year's Eve at my mother's house. She insisted on us all starting the New Year with a good hot meal, immediately after midnight, and after the first footing – usually (supposedly lucky), a tall dark man, bringing a piece of coal, bread and salt, wishing us all warmth, health and food, and getting in exchange a piece of silver and a 'Hot Toddy', to help him on his way again. Then all the family, about ten of us, did justice to my mother's enormous meat and potato pie...

This is not a modern cook book. I have tried to simplify good inexpensive recipes – some very old fashioned – to enable anyone, young or old, male or female, to cook satisfying, tasty meals.

Soups

1. Artichoke Soup
2. Carrot Soup
3. Leek Soup
4. Mushroom Soup
5. Onion Soup
6. Rabbit Broth
7. Scotch Broth
8. Dumplings

Soups

Soups can be very welcome and comforting when the weather is colder, especially if served with crunchy toast or croutons.

1.   Artichoke Soup

Ingredients

1lb [450g] Jerusalem artichokes
1 large onion, chopped
cold water, with a dessertspoon
   of lemon juice

^{1}/2pt [300ml] milk
celery salt
^{1}/2oz [15g] margarine

Method

Wash and clean the vegetables, and cut into pieces. Put into saucepan and cover with cold water and lemon juice, cover pan and simmer until tender. Put through a sieve, add milk and season with celery salt. Reheat without bringing to the boil. Add margarine just before serving. Best eaten the same day.

2.   Carrot Soup

Ingredients

1oz [25g] margarine
^{1}/2 grated carrot
1 grated onion
1^1/2pt [900ml] water

^{1}/2pt [300ml] milk
1oz [25g] flour or oatmeal
^{1}/4 teaspoon [1ml] nutmeg
salt to taste

Method

Warm margarine, add vegetables, then a little water. Cook until vegetables are soft, then add milk and thickening, and season to taste.

3.   Leek Soup

Ingredients

2 good sized leeks (white part only)
1oz [25g] margarine or butter
1/2lb [225g] peeled and thinly sliced potato
1 stick of celery chopped

seasoning
handful of rice
1 1/2pts [900ml] stock or water
grated cheese

Method

Clean vegetables well. Cut the white part of leeks in slices and fry in the margarine, add potato, celery, and seasoning. Cover with the stock and boil gently for quarter of an hour. Add the handful of rice, and simmer for 5 minutes. Then cook more slowly for 30 minutes. Put all through a sieve, and serve with grated cheese.

• • • • • • • • •

4.   Mushroom Soup

Ingredients

1/4lb [115g] finely chopped mushrooms
1oz [25g] butter
1pt [600ml] milk
1 finely chopped onion

pepper and salt
little flour to thicken
little cream, if liked

Method

Fry mushrooms and onions in butter, until tender, but not brown. Add 3/4pt milk, and pepper and salt, then simmer for half an hour. Mix flour with remaining milk, and add, stirring well. This soup is improved by addition of a little cream.

• • • • • • • • •

5.   Onion Soup

Ingredients

3 onions (minced)
1oz [25g] fat
1 tablespoon flour
1 small dessertspoon made mustard

3 teaspoons beef extract
seasoning
1 1/4pt [750ml] stock or water

Method

Lightly fry minced onions in fat for about 5 minutes. Mix in the flour and moisten with the stock. When smooth, add the beef extract, mustard and seasoning, simmer for 5 minutes and serve.

6. Rabbit Broth

Ingredients

1 rabbit
a little flour
2oz [50g] butter

2 onions, chopped
seasoning
little dried sage

Method

Cut the rabbit into joints, wash well, and dry with a cloth. Dust the joints with flour, melt the butter in a pan, and fry the rabbit in it, until brown. Place the pieces of rabbit in a stewpan and add about 2pt of boiling water, the chopped onions and seasonings. Simmer for 2 hours. Mix the flour to a paste with a little cold water. Add a cup of the boiling liquor to the paste and stir well. Pour back into the pan, stir and bring to the boil. Cook for a few minutes. Remove the rabbit from the broth, cut some of the meat off the bones into small pieces and serve with the broth. The remainder of the meat can be served separately with a brown sauce and vegetables of your choice.

· · · · · · · · ·

7. Scotch Broth

Ingredients

1 lb [450g] neck of mutton
3pt [1800ml] stock
1 large carrot
1 large onion
1 medium turnip
2 or 3 stalks celery

1 teacup of barley
1 tablespoon [15g] chopped parsley
salt
$1/2$ teaspoon [1$1/2$ml] peppercorns
   (tied in muslin)

Method

Cut up the meat in small pieces and remove the fat. Place in a stewpan with the stock, bring to the boil and skim, now add all the ingredients except parsley, the vegetables being diced, and simmer slowly for 2 hours, skimming off the fat as it rises. Boil, remove peppercorns, stir in the parsley and serve.

· · · · · · · · ·

8.   Dumplings

Dumplings are very tasty, served with any broth or soup or stews. They should be added to the dish half an hour before the dish is done.

Ingredients

^{1}/4lb [115g] flour
1^1/2oz [40g] chopped suet
salt and pepper

^{1}/2 chopped onion
^{1}/4 teaspoon baking powder

Method

Mix all the ingredients together with cold water to form a soft dough. Divide into 12 balls, flour each one and place them in the boiling liquid with the meat for 20 to 30 minutes.

• • • • • • • • •

Fish Savouries

1. Baked Steamed Cod or Haddock
2. Fish Chowder
3. Crabmeat Maryland
4. Cod and Macaroni Casserole
5. Fish Pie
6. Kedgeree
7. Mackerel
8. Skirly Herrings
9. Salmon Fritters
10. Shrimp and Egg

Fish Savouries

1. Baked Stuffed Cod or Haddock

Serves 5 or 6 portions

Ingredients

2lb [900g] middle cod
3oz [75g] breadcrumbs
1¹/₂oz [40g] chopped suet
dripping or margarine

salt and pepper
dried herbs
1 egg

Method

Clean the fish and lay it in a greased baking tin. Mix together breadcrumbs, suet, seasonings, herbs and the egg. Spread this mixture over the fish and dab with knobs of dripping or margarine. Bake for 30 minutes in a moderate oven Mark 4/350°F/180°C and serve with parsley sauce.

Ingredients for parsley sauce

1oz [25g] butter
1oz [25g] flour

¹/₂ to 1pt [300 to 600ml] milk
2 teaspoons chopped parsley

Method

Melt butter in a saucepan, stir in the flour, add the milk, stir until smooth and boil for a few minutes stirring the whole time. Then add salt and pepper to taste and 2 teaspoons chopped parsley.

Here is an American style dish, a chowder, that is simple to make and delicious.

2.   Fish Chowder

For 4 people

Ingredients

1lb [450g] cod
1pt [600ml] milk
2 medium dessert pears – peeled,
    cored and diced
2 rashers streaky bacon (diced)

nutmeg or mace to taste
1lb [450g] raw potatoes
3 sticks of celery (cut in 1" lengths)
1 medium sized onion (diced)
$^1/_4$lb [115g] peeled prawns

Method

Simmer fish in milk with nutmeg or mace for about 15 minutes. When tender, drain fish, remove bones and skin, flake fish and put on one side. Simmer potatoes, pears and celery in fish liquor until tender. Meanwhile, fry bacon with onion in a separate pan until golden brown. Add to dish containing cooked vegetables. Stir in prawns and flaked fish. Serve hot.

• • • • • • • • •

3.   Crabmeat Maryland

Serves 4 portions

Ingredients

2oz [50g] butter
1$^1/_2$ tablespoons flour
about $^1/_2$pt [300ml] milk

1 tin crab (or 6 crabsticks)
wine glass of sherry
lemon juice

Method

Melt butter in a clean pan over a gentle heat, blend with flour and gradually add milk, stirring all the time until the mixture is smooth and thick. Let this cook for about 5 minutes, then add crab (if crabsticks are used, cut up into small pieces) and stir gently so that the pieces do not break up too much. When this is heated through, add a little more milk and sherry and a few drops of lemon juice. Heat and serve on freshly made toast.

• • • • • • • • •

4.   Cod and Macaroni Casserole

Oven setting Mark 5/375°F/190°C

Ingredients

2oz [50g] macaroni
2lb [900g] cod
salt and pepper
1/2 teaspoon chopped parsley
   (or dried herbs)

3oz [75g] white breadcrumbs
1/2pt [300ml] milk
1 egg
butter

Method

Break the macaroni into pieces and place in a pan of boiling salted water. Boil for 10 minutes, then strain off the water. Wash the cod and place it in a large greased casserole. Sprinkle with the salt, pepper and chopped parsley or dried herbs. Arrange the macaroni and some of the crumbs in layers round the fish, heat the milk (not quite to the boil) and pour onto the beaten egg. Pour this over the macaroni. Sprinkle the remainder of the crumbs over the fish and macaroni. Place a few pieces of butter on top. Cover with a lid and bake for 1 hour at above oven setting. Remove the lid for the last 10 minutes to brown the crumbs.

• • • • • • • • •

5.   Fish Pie

Serves 4 or 5 portions

Ingredients

1oz [25g] butter
1oz [25g] flour
1/2pt [300ml] milk
1/2 to 3/4lb [225 to 350g] cooked white fish

1/2lb [225g] mashed potatoes
salt and pepper
2 eggs

Method

Make a sauce with flour, butter and milk, cook in saucepan over gentle heat, when thickened, add gradually cooked fish and mashed potatoes. Add salt and pepper to taste, then beaten egg yolks till all are slightly cooked. Lastly, add beaten egg whites and pour into pie dish and bake for 20 minutes or more in a medium oven Mark 5/375°F/190°C.

• • • • • • • • •

6. Kedgeree

Ingredients

2oz [50g] margarine
¹/₂lb [225g] cooked flaked fish
2oz [50g] rice (boiled till tender)

salt, pepper and nutmeg to taste
I hard boiled egg

Method

Melt margarine in a saucepan and stir in the fish and rice. Add the seasonings and chopped egg. Heat gently until thoroughly hot.

· · · · · · · · ·

7. Mackerel

How we would prize this fish if it cost as much as salmon.

Ingredients

2 medium mackerel
Dijon mustard

cold butter sauce

Method

Clean mackerel, dry and make 2 incisions in the skin of each fish and press with Dijon mustard. Open them flat and grill with butter, until they start to brown. Mix 2 egg yolks with a teaspoon of Dijon mustard, add juice of ¹/₂ lemon, add chopped parsley. Gradually stir in 3oz butter which has just melted. Serve separately.

· · · · · · · · ·

8. Skirly Herrings

Ingredients

I medium onion (sliced)
3 pairs boned herrings

3 tablespoons oatmeal
fat for frying

Method

Fry onions and oatmeal together, until golden brown. This forms the skirly. Lay 3 (cleaned and gutted) herrings, skin down in roasting tin and spread with skirly. Cover with 3 other herrings, skin uppermost and bake in medium oven Mark 5/350°F/190°C for ³/₄-1 hour.

9.   Salmon Fritters

Ingredients

¹/₂lb [225g] mashed potatoes
¹/₄lb [115g] salmon (tinned)
2oz [50g] breadcrumbs
salt and pepper

yolk of egg
chopped parsley
fat for frying

Method

Mix all the ingredients together, form into flat cakes, dip into egg and breadcrumbs and fry in very hot fat.

• • • • • • • • •

10.   Shrimp and Egg

Ingredients

1oz [25g] butter
little chopped onion
2oz [50g] shrimps

little milk, salt and pepper to taste
toasted bread to serve
1 egg

Method

Put butter in frying pan and add the onion, cook, but do not brown. Add the shrimps. Beat up the egg and milk, with seasoning to taste and add to the shrimps. When the egg is set, serve hot on toast.

• • • • • • • • •

Savouries

1.   Macaroni Carbonara

Serves 2 portions

Ingredients

¹/₂lb [225g] macaroni
¹/₄lb [115g] streaky bacon (chopped)
2 tablespoons grated Parmesan cheese
salt and freshly milled black pepper

2 large eggs
knob of butter
a little oil

Method

Before you cook the macaroni, have ready a large mixing bowl (which should be heated) in a medium oven Mark 4/350°F/180°C. Then place the macaroni in a saucepan of briskly boiling water, in which salt and a few drops of oil have been added. Cook it without a lid for about 12 minutes or more. While that is happening, melt a little oil in a frying pan and cook the bacon, not crisply, just until the fat starts to run. Also break the eggs into a bowl, season them with salt and pepper and grated Parmesan and beat them with a fork. Now put 2 plates in the oven to warm, then drain the cooked macaroni in a colander. Whip the hot bowl out of the oven and tip macaroni into it. Quickly add the bacon, followed by the beaten eggs and stir it all around speedily and deftly. Continue stirring and the eggs will soon cook and turn slightly granular from the heat of the bowl. Serve on warmed plates with a knob of butter and some Parmesan cheese.

• • • • • • • • •

2.   Scotch Eggs

Serves 4 portions

Ingredients

5 large eggs
1/2lb [225g] pork sausages
1 rounded teaspoon parsley (chopped)

salt and pepper
fat or oil for deep frying
3oz [75g] fine white breadcrumbs

Method

Make the day before. Serve cold. Put 4 eggs in a pan of cold water. Boil for 10 minutes. Drain eggs and cool in a pan of cold water. Meanwhile, skin the sausages, put sausage meat, parsley and a little salt and pepper into a bowl, mix well, then divide into 4. Shell the eggs, mould a quarter of the sausage meat around each egg. Put the fat or oil on stove to heat. Beat the remaining egg lightly. Brush the sausage-coated eggs with the beaten egg. Roll in breadcrumbs. Deep fry the eggs in hot fat for about 7 minutes until golden brown and sausage meat is cooked through. Drain well on kitchen paper. When cold, wrap in foil and store in fridge or very cold place.

• • • • • • • • •

3.   Beans and Bacon

Ingredients

1/2lb [225g] streaky bacon
1 lb [450g] tin baked beans
Worcester sauce

1 tablespoon [15ml] chopped
  parsley
salt and pepper

Method

Turn grill on to full heat, arrange bacon rashers on grid. Slightly lower heat and grill bacon for about 3 minutes until cooked, turn and grill for another 2 to 3 minutes. Meanwhile, turn beans into saucepan and heat gently. Stir in sauce to taste and parsley. Serve the bacon on the beans.

• • • • • • • •

4. Leek and Bacon Upside Down

Serves 4 portions

Ingredients

½lb [225g] long grain rice
1lb [450g] prepared leeks
salt and pepper

1oz [25g] butter
½lb [225g] streaky bacon
2 hard-boiled eggs (sliced)

Method

Cook long grain rice in sufficient salted water to be absorbed in the cooking time. Stir in the butter and keep warm. Thinly slice leeks and wash thoroughly. Blanch in boiling water for 5 minutes. Drain. Rind and dice bacon. Fry rashers until the fat starts to flow and bacon is lightly browned. Stir in the leeks and cook a few minutes longer. Adjust seasoning. Slice eggs and gently fold through the leek mixture. Turn into buttered 2½pt tin or casserole or pudding basin. Top with buttered rice. Press down lightly. Cover with foil and heat through in oven Mark 4/350°F/180°C for 20 minutes or longer. Invert on to warm dish, and serve with or without cheese sauce.

• • • • • • • • •

5. Cheese Dreams

Ingredients

slices of bread and butter
1½ to 2oz [40 to 50g] cheese
    per 2 slices of bread

little made mustard
knob of butter or lard for frying
pepper

Method

Cut bread about ¼" thick and butter it. Slice the cheese and lay it on half the slices of bread. Season the cheese with the mustard. Make into sandwiches and cut sandwiches into 4 pieces. Fry in smoking fat, pepper them and serve very hot.

• • • • • • • • •

6. Cheese Egg

Ingredients

small pieces of bacon
1 tomato
1 egg

grated cheese
salt and pepper
grease for dish

Method

Into a small greased dish place a layer of bacon and cover with a layer of tomato. Break the egg on top and cover all with a layer of grated cheese. Add seasoning to taste. Bake in a moderate oven Mark 4/350°F/180°C for about 20 minutes. This can be made in a larger dish to serve more people, with additional ingredients, and the use of an egg per person.

• • • • • • • • •

7. Cheese Soufflé

Serves 4 portions

Ingredients

1oz [25g] butter
1oz [25g] flour
1/2pt [300ml] milk
1/2 teaspoon salt

3oz [75g] grated cheese
4 egg whites
little white pepper/Cayenne pepper
3 egg yolks

Method

Mix the butter and flour over a gentle heat in a medium-sized saucepan. Add the milk and stir until it boils and thickens. Take the pan off the heat and add the seasoning. Mix well. Add the egg yolks one by one, and then the cheese. Beat the egg whites until quite stiff and stir gently into the mixture. Pour all into a buttered soufflé dish or pie dish and bake in a quick oven for 20 minutes Mark 7/425°F/220°C. Serve at once.

• • • • • • • • •

8.   Spring Chicken with Mushrooms

Ingredients

1 small chicken
1oz [25g] butter
seasoning
1 small onion

¹/₄lb [115g] mushrooms
few chillies (optional)
milk to cover
little cornflour

Method

Cut chicken into joints and fry in butter until brown. Season and add chopped onion, mushrooms, chillies. Cover with milk and simmer slowly for 35 minutes or until tender. Remove chicken, thicken sauce with cornflour and serve poured over chicken.

• • • • • • • • •

9.   Ham Toast

Ingredients

¹/₂oz [15g] butter
1 egg
little minced ham (enough to
    cover a slice of toast)

little gravy or milk, to moisten
serve on toast

Method

Melt the butter in a stewpan until slightly browned. Beat up the egg and add to the butter and also add the finely minced ham, with the gravy or milk to moisten. Stir quickly with a fork and spread on toast to serve.

• • • • • • • • •

10. Haricot Beans

Serves 4 portions

Ingredients

1lb [450g] haricot or brown beans
3oz [75g] fat bacon
1 dessertspoon black treacle
1 teaspoon dry mustard

1 teaspoon [2¹/₂ml] salt
¹/₂ teaspoon [1ml] pepper
1pt [600ml] water

Method

Soak the beans for 24 hours. Rinse, then put a layer in a deep casserole and cover with half the quantity of raw bacon. Add the remaining beans and on top put the rest of the bacon. Mix the treacle, mustard, salt, pepper and water and pour over the casserole. Cover with lid and bake slowly for about 1¹/₂ to 2 hours.

• • • • • • • • •

11. Stuffed Vegetable Marrow

Serves 4 portions

Ingredients

1 marrow
¹/₄lb [115g] finely minced cooked meat
¹/₂oz [15g] fresh breadcrumbs
¹/₂oz [15g] minced onion

1oz [25g] dripping or margarine
1 egg
tablespoon milk
seasoning

Method

Wash and peel the marrow. Cut off one end and scoop out the seeds. Mix the meat, breadcrumbs, onion, egg and milk, season with pepper and salt and press into the prepared marrow shell. Tie the end back on with tape, thus making the marrow complete again. Put in a greased baking tin and spread with dripping or margarine. Bake in a moderate oven Mark 4/350°F/180°C for about 1 hour. Serve with brown sauce or gravy.

• • • • • • • • •

12.   Baked Savoury Onions

Ingredients

2oz [50g] liver

1 rasher streaky bacon

4 Spanish onions

1/2oz [15g] breadcrumbs

1 dessertspoon chopped parsley

1/2 teaspoon mixed herbs

1/2 teaspoon grated lemon rind

2oz [50g] dripping

Method

Cut the liver and bacon into small pieces, peel the onions and boil in salted water for 10 minutes. Take out the centre of the onions. Chop 1 tablespoon of onion and add to the other ingredients. Mix well together. Stuff the onions with mixture and place in a baking tin with 2oz dripping. Bake in a moderate oven Mark 4/350°F/180°C for about 1 hour. Baste occasionally.

• • • • • • • • •

13.   Nut and Vegetable Loaf

Ingredients

1/2lb [225g] grated carrot

1/4lb [115g] brown breadcrumbs

1/4lb [115g] milled (chopped very fine) nuts

1oz [25g] vegetable fat or margarine

1 egg

1/2lb [225g] skinned and chopped
   tomatoes

onion or mixed herbs to taste

Method

Mix well together all the ingredients. Shape into a loaf and steam in a floured cloth for 1 hour. Cool and serve sliced with salad or brown in the oven to serve with cooked vegetables.

• • • • • • • • •

14. Potato Floddies

Ingredients

raw peeled potatoes (quantity dependent upon number of portions required)
seasoning
onions
little flour

Method

Grate potatoes and add grated onions and seasoning. Add a little flour and make a stiff batter. Fry in spoonful of hot fat. N.B. – May be flavoured with herbs or grated cheese or fish or minced meat can be used for variations.

• • • • • • • • •

15. Onion 'Pud'

(A favourite with the menfolk)

Ingredients

1 large chopped onion
2 tablespoons chopped suet
water, tablespoon oil
6 tablespoons [90ml] self-raising flour
1 small teaspoon salt, pepper

Method

Mix all the ingredients together (except the oil) with water, until you get a soft consistency. Pour the mixture into well oiled hot tin. Cook in hot oven Mark 7/425°F/220°C until the 'Pud' is brown. Turn if necessary to get an even colour. Serve with rich onion gravy. Serve with main course or on its own.

• • • • • • • • •

16. Scalloped Potatoes

Serves 4 portions

Ingredients

1¹/₂lb [700g] potatoes
seasoning
3oz [75g] plain flour

¹/₄lb [115g] margarine or dripping
1pt [600ml] milk

Method

Peel and slice the potatoes thinly. Well grease an oven dish, place at the bottom of dish a layer of potatoes seasoned with salt and pepper, dredge with flour and place on top a few knobs of margarine. Continue using the ingredients in this order, until all are used. Pour over the milk and cook in a hot oven Mark 6/400°F/200°C until milk boils, then reduce the heat to Mark 2/300°F/150°C and cook 1¹/₂ hours in all.

• • • • • • • • •

17. Welsh Rarebit

Ingredients

3oz [75g] grated cheese
1 teaspoon made mustard
1 tablespoon milk
2 rounds buttered toast

1 tablespoon melted butter or
    margarine
Cayenne and salt

Method

Mix the cheese, seasoning, melted fat and milk, spread evenly on the slices of toast and cook under the grill until evenly brown.

• • • • • • • • •

18.   Corn Fritters

Serves 6 portions

Ingredients

10¹/₂oz [300g] tin corn (cream style)
3oz [75g] self-raising flour
1 egg
salt and pepper

fat for frying
¹/₂lb [225g] grilled bacon rashers
3 tomatoes, halved and grilled
3 bananas, slit lengthways and fried
    in butter

Method

Mix the creamed corn with the self-raising flour and egg. Salt and pepper to season. Heat enough fat to cover the base of the frying pan and drop in dessertspoons of the mixture. Fry the fritters over a moderate heat, turn them when the undersides are golden and fry the other side. Drain the fritters on kitchen paper, then arrange them in rows, with the tomatoes between them and bacon and bananas at each end of the dish.

•••••••••

19.   Colcannon

Ingredients

cold cooked potatoes
cold cooked cabbage

salt and pepper
butter or bacon fat

Method

Mash the potatoes well with milk and little butter. Chop the cabbage finely and mix with potatoes, salt and pepper. Heat the butter or bacon fat in a frying pan. Turn the vegetable mixture into this, smooth over and flatten with a palette knife. Cook on the hotplate. When nicely brown underneath cut across and turn and brown the other side. Allow to heat through thoroughly.

•••••••••

20.   Fried Vegetable Marrow

Method

Peel the marrow, slice into quarters and remove the pips. Cut into small cubes. Heat 1 to 2oz [25 to 50g] of butter in a frying pan. Fry the marrow until tender and golden brown in colour; sprinkle with pepper and salt before serving.

21. Parsnips á la Française

Ingredients

3 or 4 parsnips
a little lemon juice
1 egg (beaten)
¹/₄lb [115g] breadcrumbs

1 dessertspoon chopped parsley
2oz [50g] butter
a little salt

Method

Peel and wash the parsnips, and if large, cut in half. Place them in plenty of boiling water containing a little salt and lemon juice; continue boiling until tender. Lift out, drain, brush them with the beaten egg, roll in crumbs and fry in the butter until they are a nice brown. Dish in a pyramid, pouring over the butter used for frying and sprinkle with parsley.

• • • • • • • • •

22. Potato Croquettes

Ingredients

1lb [450g] mashed potatoes
1 egg (beaten)
1oz [25g] butter
parsley

salt and pepper
3oz [75g] breadcrumbs
fat for frying

Method

Melt butter, mix in potatoes, salt, pepper and a little of the beaten egg. Flour the hands and form the mixture into pear shapes. Brush these over with beaten egg and roll them into the crumbs and fry them in smoking hot fat until nicely browned. Garnish with parsley.

• • • • • • • • •

23. Coq au Vin

A speciality for 4 persons

Ingredients

¹/₄lb [115g] bacon (rinded and chopped)
1 large onion, finely sliced
1 tablespoon oil
4 tablespoons [60ml] brandy
¹/₂ litre [500ml] good quality red wine
1 teaspoon [2¹/₂ml] mixed herbs
salt and pepper
pinch nutmeg

¹/₂lb [225g] mushrooms (sliced)
knob of butter
1 chicken jointed and skinned,
  e.g. 2 drumsticks, 2 thighs,
  2 wings and 4 breast pieces
3 tablespoons [45g] flour
1 tablespoon [15ml] sugar

Method

Fry bacon, mushrooms and onion in a large pot in butter and oil for 3 to 4 minutes, until lightly browned. Remove to an oven-proof casserole and fry the chicken pieces in the oil for 8 to 20 minutes until browned. Pour the brandy over the chicken and flame by igniting the liquid. Remove the chicken when the flames die down and put into casserole. Stir flour into the liquid and cook for 2 to 3 minutes, then gradually stir in the wine. Bring to the boil and cook until the sauce thickens. Add the sugar, herbs and seasoning, then pour over the chicken and vegetables. Mix together well, cover the casserole and cook in the oven at Mark 4/350°F/180°C for about 1¹/₂ hours. Serve with rice or potatoes.

● ● ● ● ● ● ● ● ●

24. Cauliflower au Gratin

Ingredients

2 small cauliflowers
$^1/_4$ teaspoon [$^1/_2$ml] pepper
a few grains Cayenne
$^1/_2$ teaspoon [1ml] salt
3oz [75g] grated Parmesan cheese

1oz [25g] butter
$^1/_4$pt [150ml] water
$^1/_4$pt [150ml] milk
1oz [25g] flour
a few drops of lemon juice

Method

Soak the cauliflowers for 1 hour in salt and water. Drain well and cut off the stems quite close. Place the flowers head-downwards in a pan of boiling water containing 1 teaspoon salt to each pint. Boil till tender for 12 to 20 minutes. Drain and set in a dish with flowers upwards. Rub the flour and butter together in a saucepan over a gentle heat until melted and mixed. Add the water, milk and seasoning, boil for 3 minutes and add half of the grated cheese. Pour this sauce over the cauliflower and sprinkle with the remainder of the cheese. Cook in the preheated oven for 10 minutes Mark 7/425°F/220°C.

• • • • • • • • •

Meats

Meats

1.   Beef Steak Pudding

Ingredients

1 lb [450g] beefsteak
¼lb [115g] kidney (optional)
¼pt [150ml] water

½lb [225g] suet pastry
1 tablespoon flour
salt and pepper

Method

Line a deep basin, which has been well greased, with suet pastry rolled ⅓" thick. Put the flour with salt and pepper on a plate. Cut the meat into strips 2½" long and 1" wide, and the fat into very small pieces. Roll each piece of meat in the seasoned flour, place a small piece of fat on the end of each piece and roll up. Place these rolls in the basin and pour the water over. Wet the edge of the pastry lining and cover with a round piece of pastry. Thoroughly seal the edges, cover with buttered paper and steam for 3 hours. Turn pudding onto a dish. N.B. When pudding is cooked, take off the buttered paper and cut a small piece from centre of the pudding. This will prevent the pudding breaking up, when turning out.

2.   Suet Pastry

Ingredients

½lb [225g] plain flour
¼lb [115g] shredded suet
½ teaspoon mixed herbs (optional)

1½ teaspoons baking powder
½ teaspoon salt
water for mixing

Method

Sift the flour, salt, baking powder, add suet and herbs and mix to a firm dough with water. Roll out to ⅓" thick, and line the greased pudding basin, leaving a good margin of dough hanging over the edge. After filling the basin with meat (as above recipe for beef steak pudding). Cover with a round piece of pastry. Wet the edges, then fold over the surplus pastry lining the basin and lay it on top. Press down firmly, so gravy does not escape.

3. Bavarian Beef Rolls

Serves 4 portions

Ingredients

1lb [450g] raw minced beef
1 tablespoon chopped parsley
1 egg
garlic if liked

1 large onion (finely chopped)
salt and pepper
¹/₂lb [225g] rice or spaghetti
olive oil for frying

Tomato sauce

1lb [450g] sliced tomatoes
2oz [50g] lean ham or bacon (cut small)
1 teaspoon sugar
1 tablespoon flour

1oz [25g] margarine or butter
1 or 2 chopped shallots
1 bay leaf and a pinch thyme
salt and pepper

Method

Rub round basin with garlic, if liked; mix beef, onion, parsley, seasoning and beaten egg. Shape into flat ovals and fry in olive oil quickly. Meanwhile, cook rice (or spaghetti) in water, with a little salt. Serve the beef rolls in one dish, and hot rice in another, covered with the tomato sauce. To make tomato sauce, melt butter (or margarine) in a pan and add ham and shallots; cook gently, not browning, add sugar, herbs and seasoning, then add the tomatoes. Sprinkle over the flour, stir and boil into sauce. Sieve and pour over the rice. N.B. Tinned tomato purée can be used instead of fresh tomatoes and the shallots can be replaced by a small finely chopped onion.

· · · · · · · · ·

4. Beef and Pork Brawn

Ingredients

1 pig's foot
sprig of thyme
1 chopped carrot
pepper and salt
sufficient water to cover

1 bay leaf, 1 onion
sprig of parsley, pinch nutmeg
¹/₂lb [225g] stewing beef
good stock

Method

Cook herbs, vegetables, pig's foot, beef and seasoning in water and simmer VERY SLOWLY, till the meat comes off the foot and beef is cooked. When cooked, bone the meat and chop altogether very finely, add sufficient stock to make a jellied mould, pour into a wetted mould and leave to set. Garnish with parsley.

5. Roast Stuffed Fillet of Veal

Ingredients

2lb [900g] fillet of veal
2oz [50g] breadcrumbs
1oz [25g] chopped suet
$^1/_2$ tablespoon chopped parsley
dripping

$^1/_2$ teaspoon mixed dried herbs
a little grated lemon rind
egg or milk for mixing
seasoning

Method

Bone the meat and stuff with forcemeat (made with breadcrumbs, suet, parsley, herbs, lemon and seasoning, mixed with sufficient beaten egg or milk to hold together). Tie securely into a good shape. Place it in a baking tin with a piece of dripping, and bake for 2 hours at Mark 7/425°F/220°C, basting occasionally.

• • • • • • • • •

6. Irish Stew

Ingredients

2lb [900g] neck or scraps of mutton
2lb [900g] potatoes
2 large onions

$^3/_4$pt [450ml] water
$^1/_4$ teaspoon salt
$^1/_4$ teaspoon pepper

Method

Divide the meat into neat pieces, cut up the potatoes roughly and slice the onions. Place in a casserole alternate layers of meat, potatoes and onions with a good sprinkling of salt and pepper between the layers, pour in the water and cover tightly. Cook in a very low oven for 4 hours at Mark $^1/_4$/150°F/70°C.

• • • • • • • • •

7. Stuffed Breast of Lamb

Ingredients

Lean breast of lamb or mutton   little vinegar

Stuffing

2oz [50g] breadcrumbs   1oz [25g] suet
pepper and salt   1 dessertspoon chopped parsley
1 teaspoon sweet herbs   grated rind of ¹/₂ lemon
1 egg to bind

Method

Remove the bones from the meat and wipe it over with a little vinegar. Prepare the stuffing by mixing all the ingredients together, binding with the beaten egg. Spread this over the breast. Roll up tightly and skewer and bake in a moderate oven Mark 4/350°F/180°C for about 1¹/₂ hours.

• • • • • • • • •

8. Hamburgers

Serves 8 portions

Ingredients

1lb [450g] minced beef, or half minced beef,   1 tablespoon green tomato chutney
    plus any left over meat game or poultry   pinch of salt
1 teaspoon Worcester sauce   fried tomatoes and onion rings for
fat for frying   garnishing

Method

Mix all the ingredients well together and divide into eight portions. Shape into flat cakes and fry quickly in a frying pan, browning both sides. Lower the heat and cook slowly for 30 minutes, turning occasionally. Serve with fried tomatoes and fried onion rings.

• • • • • • • • •

9.   Kidney Dish

Serves 4 portions

Ingredients
4 kidneys
small piece of bacon
a little flour, pepper and salt
a little water

¹/₄lb [115g] macaroni
seasoning and a little butter
2oz [50g] grated cheese

Method
Cut the kidneys in slices and fry in a pan for about 5 minutes with a small piece of bacon. Remove the kidneys, add the flour, salt and pepper, and a little water, stir until it thickens, then add the kidneys. Simmer gently for about 20 minutes. Boil the macaroni for about 20 minutes. When tender, strain and dry and add a little butter, seasoning and grated cheese. Make quite hot and put round the outside of a dish, with the kidneys in the centre.

• • • • • • • • •

10.   Curried Mutton

Ingredients
1 tablespoon coconut
2lb [900g] neck of mutton
2oz [50g] butter
1 onion
1 small apple
1 tablespoon curry powder

2oz [50g] flour
¹/₂pt [300ml] good stock
2oz [50g] sultanas
¹/₂ teaspoon sugar
¹/₂ teaspoon salt
1 tablespoon lemon juice

Method
Steep the coconut in a little boiling water (keep water). Remove the bones from the meat and divide into 1" squares. Fry the meat until brown with butter in a pan. Remove the meat and fry the onions and apple (peeled and chopped up). Sprinkle in the curry powder and flour and fry for a few minutes. Gradually add the stock, stirring to a thick, smooth mixture. Turn into a casserole with the rest of the ingredients, including the water strained from the coconut. Cover with lid and cook in the oven at Mark 3/325°F/160°C for 1¹/₂ to 2 hours. Dish in a pile with the sauce around and serve with a dish of boiled rice.

• • • • • • • • •

11.　　　Pig's Feet in Batter

Ingredients

2 pig's feet
1/4lb [115g] flour
1 egg

1/4pt [150ml] milk
pepper and salt
fat for frying

Method

Boil pig's feet until tender. Pour off liquid and reserve. Take out all the bones and chop flesh into small pieces. Add pepper and salt to taste and a little of the liquid in which they were boiled. Pour onto a dish to a thickness of about 1/2" and leave until cold. Make a batter of the flour, egg and milk. Cut meat into pieces, dip in batter and fry in shallow fat on both sides until brown.

· · · · · · · · ·

12.　　　Welsh Pie

Ingredients

1lb [450g] boiled potatoes
2 tablespoons hot milk
3 tablespoons grated cheese

pepper and salt
1 tablespoon butter
breadcrumbs

Method

Mash the potatoes with the milk and mix in cheese and seasoning. Cover the bottom of a pie dish with fine breadcrumbs, having first buttered the pie dish well. Add potato mixture and bake in a hot oven Mark 7/425°F/220°C for half an hour or more. Serve with sweetened vinegar.

· · · · · · · · ·

13. Delicious Rabbit

Ingredients

1 rabbit	4 cloves
salt and pepper	mixed herbs
vinegar	1/4pt [150ml] water
2oz [50g] margarine	1 teaspoon sugar
1/2lb [225g] chopped onion	flour for thickening

Method

Wash and cut up the rabbit and put in a basin, sprinkle with salt and pepper and cover with vinegar. Stand overnight. Melt margarine in a pan. Add the rabbit, also the chopped raw onions, the cloves and a sprinkling of herbs, 1/4pt of water and the vinegar in which the rabbit was soaked. Let the pan simmer for 1 1/2 hours, stirring now and again. Thicken with flour before serving, and add 1 teaspoon sugar.

• • • • • • • •

12. Sweet and Sour Pork

Serves 4 portions

Ingredients

1lb [450g] pork	1/3 cup vinegar
1/3 cup of sugar	1/2 cup white wine
1 small teaspoon ginger	2 tablespoons, soy sauce
2 tablespoons cornflour	1 egg
1/2oz [15g] flour	2 pineapple rings (chopped)
1 cup water	oil for frying
1/4lb [115g] tomatoes (chopped very small)	

Method

Mix water with cornflour to a smooth paste, add sugar, vinegar, wine, ginger, Soy sauce, tomato and mix well. Cut pork into thin strips. Coat with beaten egg and flour. Fry in oil, a few at a time, and keep hot on a plate. Add pineapple to sauce mixture. Bring to the boil and simmer until it thickens. Pour sauce over meat and serve with boiled or fried rice.

• • • • • • • •

15. Chicken Breast with White Sauce

Serves 4 portions

Ingredients

2 whole chicken breasts
I large onion, chopped
I small tin mushrooms (sliced)
milk to blend

2 tablespoons flour
salt and pepper
knob of butter
I tablespoon oil

Method

Clean and dry chicken, and lay in oiled fireproof pie dish, sprinkle with salt and pepper, and cook in moderate oven for about 45 minutes. Put a chopped onion in a saucepan and cover with water. Cook until tender and water has almost evaporated. Blend the flour with butter and milk, stir well into the onions until creamy, adding more milk if necessary. Add mushrooms, salt and pepper to taste. Pour over the chicken and serve hot with mashed potatoes and peas or serve cold next day with mixed green salad. (But remember the rules about cooling and storing meat properly.)

• • • • • • • • •

16. Chicken with Almonds

Serves 3 to 4 portions

Ingredients

2 chicken joints
I tablespoon dry sherry
I large egg white
I level teaspoon cornflour

$1/4$ teaspoon ground ginger
4 large mushrooms
2 tablespoons corn oil
2oz [50g] skinned almonds

Method

Bone and skin chicken. Cut meat into $1/2$" cubes. Mix sherry with egg white, cornflour and ginger. Soak chicken in this for 15 minutes. Wash and slice mushrooms, fry chicken in oil for 5 minutes, stirring. Add mushrooms, cook 2 minutes more, still stirring. Add nuts. Cook for 20 minutes longer, slowly. Serve at once.

Hot Puddings

Hot Puddings

Try something different. These sweets are delicious.

1. Apple Meringue Pudding

Serves 4 portions

Ingredients

1lb [450g] peeled and cored cooking apples
sugar to taste
½oz [15g] margarine

1 egg yolk
1oz [25g] custard powder
2 tablespoons water

Meringue

1 egg white

2oz [50g] sugar

Method

Stew apples until soft, and sweeten to taste. Add margarine. Mix egg yolk, custard powder and water, to make a thin cream. Add to the apples and cook until thick, about 4 minutes. Put in a pie dish and when cool, cover with meringue and bake in a slow oven at Mark 4/350°F/180°C until meringue is set and crisp – about half an hour. May be served with custard or cream. To make meringue: whisk egg white until it stands in peaks, add half the sugar, whisk again until stiff, add the remainder of the sugar and fold in with a metal spoon.

2. Banana Pudding

Serves 3 to 4 portions

Ingredients

3oz [75g] sugar
3oz [75g] margarine
1 egg
6oz [175g] flour

½ teaspoon baking powder
⅛pt [75ml] milk
3 thinly sliced bananas

Method

Cream the sugar and margarine and add the egg, beaten. Work in the flour and baking powder with the milk and lastly, the thinly sliced bananas. Steam for 1½ hours and serve with custard.

3.   Baked Jam Roll

Serves 6 portions
A lovely satisfactory sticky 'Pud', to suit all but the slimmers.

Ingredients

³/₄lb [350g] plain flour
pinch of salt
12 to 14 tablespoons cold water
a little milk to glaze
to serve, caster sugar and custard

1 level teaspoon baking powder
6oz [175g] shredded suet
4 rounded tablespoons
   strawberry jam

Method

Sift flour, baking powder, and salt into a bowl, stir in the suet and mix with water to make a fairly soft dough. Knead lightly, then roll on to a lightly floured surface and shape into a rectangle. Spread with jam to within ¹/₂ inch of edges. Dampen all edges and roll up lightly from the short end. Seal edges well and put on a greased baking sheet, brush with milk and cook in a hot oven Mark 6/400°F/200°C for about 50 minutes until lightly golden.

● ● ● ● ● ● ● ● ●

4.   Apple Sponge Pudding

Ingredients

2 medium sized apples (peeled and cored)
1 teaspoon water and a little sugar
   to sweeten apples
2oz [50g] margarine

2oz [50g] sugar
1 egg
2oz [50g] self-raising flour

Method

Butter a pudding dish and slice in the apples, sprinkle with sugar and taste. Add the teaspoon water. Cream margarine and sugar, then add beaten egg and flour. Pour this mixture over the apples and cook on middle shelf at Mark 5/365°F/190°C for 40 minutes.

● ● ● ● ● ● ● ● ●

5. Bread and Butter Pudding

Serves 4 to 6 portions

Ingredients

3 slices of bread and butter (taken from large white loaf)
³/₄pt [450ml] milk
grated nutmeg

1¹/₂oz [40g] caster sugar
2oz [50g] sultanas
2 eggs
pouring cream if liked

Method

Cut slices of bread in half, put in layers in a buttered 1¹/₂pt pie dish with sugar and sultanas, finishing with bread (buttered side up). Heat milk (without boiling), and pour over lightly beaten eggs, whisking. Strain into pie dish, sprinkle with a little grated nutmeg and stand for 30 to 40 minutes. Then cook in a moderate oven at Mark 4/350°F/180°C for 40 or 50 minutes, until set and golden brown.

• • • • • • • • •

6. Caramel Pudding

Ingredients

3oz [75g] butter
2 heaped tablespoons sugar
2 eggs

4 tablespoons flour
1¹/₂ teaspoons baking powder
3 tablespoons golden syrup

Method

Mix butter to a cream, add sugar and beaten eggs, then flour and baking powder. Grease pint-sized pudding basin and put in the syrup. Add the mixture and steam for 3 hours.

• • • • • • • • •

7. Chocolate Favourite Pudding (A Winner)

Serves 6 portions

Ingredients

3 thick slices of white bread and butter
¹/₂oz [15g] cocoa
1 egg yolk

2oz [50g] sugar
1pt [600ml] milk

Meringue Topping

white of an egg
2oz [50g] sugar

pinch of salt

Method

Cut bread into cubes, place in a fireproof dish. Mix sugar, cocoa, egg yolk, and a little of the milk into a paste and pour over the bread. Add the rest of the milk, and cook in a medium oven Mark 4/350°F/180°C, until dark brown. Remove from oven, beat the white of the egg very stiffly with a good pinch of salt. Stir in the sugar and place in teaspoonfuls on the top of the pudding. Return to oven to brown.

• • • • • • • • •

8. Chocolate Soufflé Pudding

Ingredients

1¹/₂oz [40g] chocolate powder
1 tablespoon cornflour
1 level tablespoon flour
1 egg

1¹/₂pt [900ml] milk
2oz [50g] sugar
1¹/₂oz [40g] butter or margarine

Method

Mix together chocolate powder, cornflour and flour. Beat egg and a little of the milk together. Mix this smoothly into chocolate powder. Boil remainder of the milk with 2oz sugar and 1¹/₂oz butter in a pan. Bring to the boil and pour on to the mixture, stirring well. Pour back into pan, and let it come to the boil, stirring well all the time. Pour into a pie dish and put into a slow oven Mark 2/300°F/150°C for 25 minutes.

• • • • • • • • •

9. Apricot Charlotte

Ingredients
1/2lb [225g] dried apricots
6oz [175g] sugar

1/2lb [225] breadcrumbs
2oz [50g] butter or margarine

Method
Wash the apricots and soak in cold water for 12 hours. Butter a pie dish and put in alternate layers of fruit, breadcrumbs and sugar, making breadcrumbs the top layer. Put the butter in small pieces on top of the pudding and cover with buttered paper. Cook in preheated oven Mark 5/375°F/190°C for 1 hour.

• • • • • • • • •

10. Baked Date Pudding

Serves 4 portions

Ingredients
6oz [175g] dry bread
2oz [50g] margarine
1oz [25g] sugar
2 tablespoons grated carrot

1/4lb [115g] dates
1 teaspoon baking powder
milk to mix

Method
Soak bread in cold water for a few minutes and squeeze as dry as possible. Beat margarine and sugar to a cream, add grated carrot, bread, and chopped dates and baking powder. Add sufficient milk to make a fairly soft consistency. Put into a greased dish and bake in a moderate oven Mark 4/350°F/180°C for about 3/4 hour, or until risen and brown. Serve with custard sauce.

• • • • • • • • •

11.   Spotted Dick

Serves 6 portions

Ingredients

¹/₂lb [225g] self-raising flour
pinch of salt
1 level teaspoon baking powder
¹/₄lb [115g] shredded suet

3oz [85g] caster sugar
3oz [85g] currants
3oz [85g] sultanas
milk to mix

Method

Half fill a large saucepan with cold water and bring to the boil. Sprinkle some flour (not from measured out amount) on a large pudding cloth or a clean tea towel. Sift flour and baking powder into a bowl. Add suet, sugar, currants and sultanas. Add enough milk to mix to a soft dough. Put on to the prepared cloth, shape into a roll and roll up loosely. Tie ends with string and boil for 3 hours. Remove cloth carefully. Serve hot with custard.

· · · · · · · · ·

12.   Crispy Delight

Ingredients

¹/₂" thick squares of bread
    (1 to 2 per person)
honey or brown sugar

lemon juice
butter or margarine
apples, peeled, cored and sliced

Method

Remove the crusts from the bread, spread butter or margarine on each side, and put into a well greased oven dish. Cover each square of bread with sliced apples. Press well on to the bread. Sprinkle with a little lemon juice to preserve the colour, then spoon over them honey or brown sugar. Cover with a buttered paper and bake for 20 minutes in a moderate oven Mark 4/350°F/180°C.

Cold Sweets

Cold Sweets

1. Apricot Cream

Ingredients

1 small tin apricots
1 white of egg
3oz [75g] sugar
³/₄oz [21g] gelatine

¹/₂pt [300ml] cream (or rather more
than ¹/₄pt [150ml] cream and less
than ¹/₄pt [150ml] milk and water)
1 teaspoon lemon juice

Method

Strain the juice from the apricots and soak the gelatine in this, with the lemon juice. Pass the apricots through a sieve. Dissolve the gelatine in the juice, with the sugar. Beat the cream and the milk, or water, together until thick. Stir carefully together the purée, whipped cream, juice and gelatine, which must be nearly cold. Lastly, add the stiffly whipped white of egg. Stir together lightly, turn into a damp mould and leave to set. When set, turn out, and if liked, place chopped apricots round the base of the cream.

2. Banana Cream

Ingredients

3 bananas
3 tablespoons caster sugar (level)
1 packet jelly

3 tablespoons cream (tinned or
fresh)

Method

Make jelly (as per packet instructions), and leave to partly set. Beat up bananas and sugar until creamy and add cream. Beat again and add this mixture to the jelly. Whisk all together and put in a mould to set.

3. Cup Custard

Ingredients

3 eggs (leaving out 2 whites)
³/₄pt [450ml] milk

1oz [25g] sugar
flavouring

Method

Beat the egg yolks and add the milk hot, but not boiling. Beat together, turn into a jug and stand in a saucepan of water, or use a double saucepan. Place over a burner and stir until the mixture thickens, using only a small flame to avoid curdling the custard; add the sugar and the flavouring. Turn into a basin to cool. Remove the skin and serve in cups or a dish.

· · · · · · · · ·

4. Chocolate Marie

Serves 4 to 5 portions

Ingredients

4 egg whites
¹/₂lb [225g] slab chocolate

3 tablespoons water

Method

Whisk the egg whites till they stand on their own. Melt the chocolate in the water, then fold in the whites. Leave in a cool place for 2 hours before serving.

· · · · · · · · ·

5. Chocolate Mousse

Ingredients (per adult person)

1 fresh egg

1oz [25g] plain chocolate

Method

Scrape the chocolate (not too finely) into a basin, over a pan of boiling water, till soft. The basin should be big enough to hold the beaten whites of as many eggs as are being used. Separate the egg yolks and the whites and beat the whites until they are very stiff. Beat the yolks slightly and add to the melted chocolate. Mix quickly and thoroughly and then lightly fold in the beaten egg whites. Transfer to individual dishes and leave for about 3 hours in a cool place, not a refrigerator.

Moonshine Sweet

Ingredients

I heaped tablespoon cornflour
6oz [175g] caster sugar
2 egg yolks
3/4pt [450ml] pint crushed pineapple

1/8pt [75ml] cold water
1/2pt [300ml] pineapple juice
2 egg whites, stiffly beaten

Lemon Topping

1/2lb [225g] caster sugar
pinch of cream of tartar
dessertspoon lemon juice

2 level dessertspoons powdered
  gelatine
1/2pt [300ml] cold water

Method

Mix together cornflour, water, sugar and pineapple juice. Stir over heat, until it boils, then add crushed pineapple, egg yolks and whites. Pour into a dish and cover with lemon topping. To make lemon topping: mix all ingredients together, boil for 5 minutes, cool and then add lemon juice. Beat until creamy and pour over the sweet.

• • • • • • • • •

A Sweet for that Special Occasion

7. Charlotte Russe

Serves 6 to 8 portions

Ingredients

I packet lemon jelly
2 tablespoons lemon juice
1 1/4pt [750ml] milk
I vanilla pod
few diamonds of angelica
6 tablespoons water
2 1/2pt charlotte dish or mould

2 level tablespoons gelatine
  (2 sachets)
3 egg yolks
2oz [50g] caster sugar
I packet (18) sponge finger biscuits
1/4pt [150ml] whipping cream

Method

Make up the lemon jelly (as directed on packet), substituting 2 tablespoons of the water with 2 tablespoons of lemon juice. Lightly oil base of the dish, then pour jelly in to a depth of 1/3" and allow to set. Meanwhile, heat the milk in a saucepan with the vanilla pod until it is barely simmering. Remove from the heat and leave to infuse for 10 to 15 minutes. Arrange a pattern of angelica diamonds over the set jelly, then carefully spoon over a little more of the liquid jelly to set the pattern. Place the rest of the jelly in a basin to set.

Put the water in a small basin, sprinkle the gelatine on top, and leave to swell and become spongy. Transfer milk to a jug, beat the yolks and sugar, and pour in half of vanilla-flavoured milk. Return to the pan and cook over gentle heat until the custard coats the back of a wooden spoon. Remove from the heat. Add the gelatine and stir to dissolve. Stir in the rest of the vanilla-flavoured milk, after removing the pod; leave to cool until half set. Meanwhile trim the sponge finger biscuits down each side and arrange side by side, around the dish, if necessary, spreading a tiny dot of butter on the biscuits to secure in place.

When the custard is half set, lightly whip the cream, until it is floppy and fold into the custard. Turn at once into the dish. If necessary trim the sponge fingers level with the mixture and place the trimmings over the top. Chill until set, turn out as for a jelly and decorate with rest of jelly, which has been chopped.

• • • • • • • • •

8.   Mince Tart

Ingredients

3oz [85g] margarine   3oz [85g] sugar (caster preferable)
2oz [50g] lard   1 egg
1/2lb [225g] flour   mincemeat

Method

Rub fat into flour, add sugar and beaten egg. Line a flan tin with thinly rolled out pastry. Add layer of mincemeat and cover with pastry. Cook in medium oven Mark 5/375°F/190°C for 25 to 30 minutes. Sprinkle with caster sugar. Serve cold with cream.

• • • • • • • • •

9.   Meringues

Ingredients
whites of 3 eggs
6oz [175g] caster sugar

a few drops of lemon juice
$1/2$ teaspoon vanilla essence

Method
Whip the whites very stiffly, fold in lightly the sugar, also the essence and lemon juice. Put into forcing bag and squeeze into egg shape on to a tin previously brushed with oil and lightly dusted with flour. (If you do not have a forcing bag, put in spoonfuls on to the baking tray, greased and floured lightly.) Put in the oven for 2 hours at Mark $1/4$/125°F/65°C. When cold, spread thickly with whipped cream nicely flavoured. Stick two together and serve. If preferred, meringues may be removed from the tin at the end of $1 1/2$ hours, the centres pushed in, and the meringues put back into the oven to dry thoroughly for half an hour.

A Quicker Method
Bake for 30 minutes at Mark 1/275°F/140°C. Then slip the meringues off the tin with a knife. Turn over on to a cake rack. Sprinkle with sugar. Replace in the oven for another half an hour at the same temperature.

• • • • • • • • •

10.   Tranby Cream

Ingredients
1pt [600ml] milk
6oz [175g] sugar
$1/2$oz [15g] gelatine

2 lemons
2 eggs

Method
Put milk, gelatine and the lemon rind into a pan. Let it remain, until flavoured. Strain into a basin and add the yolks of eggs, not much beaten. Return to the pan, and let it come to the boil, stirring all the time. Return to the basin. Beat whites of eggs into a stiff froth and stir in quickly. Add lemon juice last. Pour into a mould, whilst hot, and put into a cool place at once.

• • • • • • • • •

11.   Spanish Cream

Ingredients

1pt [600ml] milk

2 eggs

2oz [50g] sugar

1 teaspoon vanilla essence

$^1/_2$oz [15g] gelatine

$^1/_8$pt [75ml] water

Method

Heat the milk to just under boiling point and add egg yolks beaten with 1oz of sugar and vanilla. Beat whites till stiff, beat in 1oz of sugar. Dissolve gelatine in water, and add to the milk mixture. When at about blood heat, stir occasionally till at setting point. Pour into wetted mould or 6 individual dishes.

• • • • • • • • •

12.   Summer Pudding

Ingredients

slices of bread and butter, fruit stewed

Method

Line a greased basin with slices of bread and butter, which must be fitted closely together. Pour in some stewed fruit to half fill the basin. Put in a round of bread and butter and fill up with more fruit. Cover with bread and butter. Place a saucer over the top with a weight on it and leave to stand until next day. Turn out and serve with cup custard (see recipe). If liked, may be steamed for 1 hour and served hot with cream.

• • • • • • • • •

Something to impress

13.   Soufflé au Sabayon

Serves 6 or more portions

Ingredients
3 eggs
3oz [85g] caster sugar
juice of 2 and rind of 1 lemon

¹/₂pt [300ml] cream
vanilla essence
¹/₂oz gelatine in ¹/₈pt [75ml] wine
jelly or ¹/₄pt [150ml] stiff wine jelly

Method
Whisk the egg yolks, caster sugar and lemon juice over boiling water till thick and light. Add the grated rind and let this cool. Whisk the cream, dissolve gelatine in the wine (or melt jelly and whisk till nearly cold). Lastly, whip whites of egg very stiffly. Add gelatine mixture (or jelly) to the cooled yolks and fold into the cream, then fold in the whites. The mixture should set almost at once. Just before it sets, fill into small or large dishes as required. When set, decorate tastefully. Roses of cream forced round the sides looks well with a rim of crushed violets on the top.

· · · · · · · · ·

14.   Strawberry Snow

Ingredients
¹/₄lb [115g] strawberries (fresh or frozen)
1 white of egg

¹/₂oz [15g] sugar (or to taste)

Method
Save a few strawberries for decorating. Squash the remainder, add the sugar and mix. Beat the egg white until quite stiff. Put a little of the strawberry mixture into custard glasses; fold the remaining mixture into the egg and pile on top of the glasses. Decorate with cut strawberries. This is sufficient for 2 to 3 portions, and is a good way of using up over-ripe strawberries.

· · · · · · · · ·

Biscuits and Cookies

Biscuits and Cookies

1. Abbey Biscuits

Ingredients
1/4lb [115g] flour
6oz [175g] sugar
2 1/2oz [65g] coconut
2 1/2oz [65g] Quaker Oats

1 good dessertspoon Golden Syrup
2oz [50g] butter or margarine
1 dessertspoon hot water
1 level teaspoon bicarbonate of soda

Method
Mix together all the dry ingredients. Melt the syrup and fat and add the water, mix all together and bake in little dabs on a greased baking tin in a medium oven Mark 5/375°F/190°C. This quantity makes 30 small biscuits

2. Almond Slices

Ingredients
6oz [175g] self-raising flour
3oz [85g] butter
1 yolk of egg

2 teaspoons sugar
jam

Method
Rub the butter into the flour, mix in the sugar, mix with beaten egg. Roll out and line a greased swiss roll tin with pastry and spread with jam.

Filling (Spread Evenly)
2 egg whites
3oz [85g] icing sugar

a few chopped almonds
2oz [50g] ground almonds

Method
Beat the egg whites until stiff and add sugar and ground almonds. Mix well, spread evenly over pastry and put a few chopped almonds on top. Bake in a moderate oven Mark 4/350°F/180°C for 25 to 30 minutes.

3. Cherry Fingers

Ingredients

3oz [85g] sugar
1¹/₂oz [40g] margarine
cherries
1 egg

5oz [150g] self-raising flour
vanilla essence
2¹/₂oz [65g] lard
porridge oats – to sprinkle

Method

Cream fats and sugar, add the well beaten egg, a few drops of vanilla essence and the flour. Beat mixture well and spread in a shallow tin, well greased (approximately 12" by 8". Brush the top of the mixture with cold water, and sprinkle with porridge oats. Bake in a moderate oven for 20 minutes (Mark 5/375°C/190°C). Cut into fingers and put a piece of glace cherry in centre of each. Remove from tin when cold.

● ● ● ● ● ● ● ●

4. Cherry Macaroons

Ingredients – Sweet Paste Base

¹/₄lb [115g] plain flour
1oz [25g] sugar

2¹/₂oz [65g] fat
1 egg

Method

Mix as for pastry and roll into biscuits about 2" diameter. Put in a greased tin.

Ingredients – Topping

1 large egg white
¹/₄lb [115g] sugar
2oz [50g] ground almonds

¹/₄oz [7g] ground rice
1oz [25g] chopped glace cherries for
  decoration

Method

Whisk egg white very stiff, adding sugar gradually. Gently stir in other ingredients and put a small spoonful upon each biscuit. Top with a piece of cherry. Bake slowly Mark 2/300°F/150°C, makes about eighteen.

● ● ● ● ● ● ● ●

5. Cheese Biscuits

Ingredients

2oz [50g] grated cheese
2oz [50g] plain flour

2oz [50g] margarine

Method

Rub all the ingredients together till they form a firm paste (add no liquid). Roll out thin and cut into shapes. Bake in a moderate oven Mark 4/350°F/180°C till pale gold, about 10 minutes. Makes about 24 biscuits.

• • • • • • • • •

6. Rich Chocolate Biscuits

Ingredients

¹/₄lb [115g] margarine
6oz [175g] flour
1 egg

¹/₄lb [115g] sugar
pinch of salt
2oz [50g] chocolate powder or
    2 level tablespoons of cocoa

Filling

3 tablespoons ground almonds
Vanilla essence if liked
walnuts for decoration

2 tablespoons apricot jam
chocolate icing

Method

Cream fat and sugar and work in beaten egg. Add the dry ingredients and knead into a firm paste. Roll out rather thinly. Cut into rounds with a small cutter. Bake on greased oven sheet at Mark 5/375°F/190°C. Mix together the filling ingredients and when the biscuits are cool, pair them with this mixture. Ice with rather stiff chocolate icing, swirling a teaspoon on each complete biscuit and press down with half a walnut (sufficient for 24 biscuits).

• • • • • • • • •

7.   Coconut Shortbread

I flan tin, greased

Ingredients

¹/₄lb [115g] butter
1 teaspoon vanilla essence
2oz [50g] sugar
pinch of salt

¹/₄lb [115g] rolled oats
¹/₄lb [115g] coconut
1 teaspoon baking powder

Method

Melt the butter and mix into other ingredients. Press mixture down into a flan tin. Bake in a slow oven Mark 2/300°F/150°C about ³/₄ hour, cut when still warm, but leave in the tin until quite cold.

• • • • • • • • •

8.   Cream Biscuits

Ingredients

2oz [50g] margarine
1 teaspoon vanilla essence
1 level teaspoon of bicarbonate of soda
2oz [50g] sugar

1 dessertspoon syrup
2oz [50g] lard
6oz [175g] self-raising flour
butter cream for filling

Method

Cream margarine, lard, sugar and syrup. Add the bicarbonate of soda and vanilla essence, stir in the flour. Roll into small balls about the size of a marble and place on a greased baking tray. Flatten with a fork and bake in a moderate oven Mark 4/350°F/180°C for about 15 minutes. When cold, stick together with butter cream.

For the Butter Cream

Sift 2oz [50g] icing sugar, and mix 1oz [25g] butter or margarine. Beat well together and use as filling.

• • • • • • • • •

9. American Breakfast Biscuits

Ingredients

1 lb [450g] flour
1 teaspoon baking powder
3oz [85g] butter
1/2pt [300ml] milk

1oz [25g] caster sugar
a little salt
1 egg

Method

Mix the baking powder with the flour, rub in the butter, add the sugar and salt and mix into a light dough, with the beaten egg and the milk. Divide into 6. Roll out 1/2" thick, prick with a fork and bake for 20 minutes at Mark 7/425°F/220°C.

• • • • • • • • •

10. Scotch Shortbread

Ingredients

1/2lb [225g] butter
6oz [175g] caster sugar
1 teaspoon baking powder

2oz [50g] rice flour
14oz [400g] best pastry flour

Method

Mix well together the butter and sugar, sift in the flour, rice flour and baking powder. Knead well together, divide into two, roll out or knead on to a sheet of white paper. Pinch around the edges with the fingers and thumb. Prick all over with a fork. Place with the paper on the baking sheet, and bake in the oven for 40 minutes at Mark 3/325°F/170°C. Leave cakes on the paper until firm.

• • • • • • • • •

11. Viennese Creams

Ingredients

10oz [275g] margarine
7ozs [200g] sugar

3/4lb [350g] flour
vanilla essence

Method

Cream the margarine and sugar, until fluffy. Beat in the flour and a few drops of essence, pipe on to a greased baking sheet and bake at Mark 6/400°F/200°C for about 10 to 15 minutes.

12.   Rolled Wafers

To serve with ice cream or any cold sweet

Ingredients

2 eggs

pinch of salt

weight of 1 egg in sieved flour

juice and grated rind of $1/2$ lemon

weight of 1 egg in sifted sugar

little butter or margarine

Method

Whip the eggs till light and foamy. Well beat in the sugar, flour and other ingredients. Take large saucerfuls and spread out quite thinly on a greased baking sheet. Bake in a fairly hot oven Mark 6/400°F/200°C until a nice gold colour. Roll the wafers around the handle of a wooden spoon, straight from the hot tin. Leave until cold.

• • • • • • • • •

13.   Shrewsbury Biscuits

Ingredients

$1/4$lb [115g] butter

$1/4$lb [115g] sugar

1 egg

6oz [175g] flour

$1/2$ teaspoon cinnamon

1 teaspoon caraway seeds (optional)

Method

Beat the butter and sugar to a cream, add the flour, seeds and enough of the beaten egg to make a stiff paste, roll out, cut in rounds and bake on a greased oven sheet at Mark 3/325°F/170°C for 30 minutes.

• • • • • • • • •

14.   Melting Moments

Ingredients

2¹/₂oz [65g] lard
1¹/₂oz [40g] margarine
¹/₄lb [115g] sugar
¹/₂ teaspoon baking powder

5oz [150g] flour
few drops vanilla essence
porridge oats or corn flakes
cherries

Method

Cream the fats and sugar, add the essence, flour and baking powder, gradually. Wet the hands, then mould the mixture into balls, flatten them, dip them in oats or corn flakes and decorate the top with half a cherry. Bake in a moderate oven Mark 4/350°F/180°C for 15 to 20 minutes.

● ● ● ● ● ● ● ● ●

15.   Nut Fancies

Ingredients

2oz [50g] butter
paper cases
¹/₂oz [15g] ground nuts
almond essence

2¹/₂oz [65g] flour
2oz [50g] caster sugar
1 egg
pinch of baking powder

Butter Icing

1oz [25g] butter

2oz [50g] icing sugar

Method

Beat butter and sugar to a cream, add a beaten egg and flour mixed with baking powder, alternatively. Lastly, add nuts and essence. Bake at Mark 5/375°F/190°C in paper cases for about 15 minutes. When cold, spread with butter icing and chopped nuts.

● ● ● ● ● ● ● ● ●

16.   Shortbread Biscuits

Ingredients

3oz [75g] butter
3 dessertspoons sugar

7oz [200g] flour
glace cherries

Method

Beat butter and sugar to a cream, add flour and mix well. Roll out and cut into shapes, decorate with cherries. Bake in moderate oven Mark 4/350°F/180°C for about 20 minutes. Approximately 26 biscuits.

• • • • • • • • •

17.   Wholemeal Biscuits

Ingredients

1oz [25g] butter
pinch of bicarbonate soda
$^1/_4$pt [150ml] milk (warm)

$^1/_4$lb [115g] wholemeal flour
1oz [25g] caster sugar
$^1/_4$ teaspoon salt

Method

Dissolve butter and bicarbonate soda in the warm milk, mix the flour, sugar and salt together, add the milk, mix the whole into a stiff paste. Roll out thinly, cut into rounds, pierce all over with a fork, place on a greased tin and bake for 25 minutes at Mark 4/350°F/180°C.

• • • • • • • • •

18.   Cinnamon Butter Biscuits

Ingredients
6oz [175g] butter
1/2lb [225g] plain flour
1oz [25g] granulated sugar

1/4lb [115g] caster sugar
1 level teaspoon cinnamon
a little granulated sugar for coating

Method
Set the oven to warm, Mark 3/325°F/170°C. Cream the butter and sugar in a bowl until soft and fluffy. Blend in the flour and cinnamon, using your hands, knead lightly until smooth. Divide the dough into two, then roll and shape into two 6" sausages. Roll in granulated sugar to coat, wrap in foil and chill in the fridge until firm or until needed. Cut each sausage into 16 slices and place on greased baking sheets, allowing room for them to spread. Bake above the centre of the oven for 25 minutes, or until the edges of the biscuits are a light golden brown.

• • • • • • • • •

19.   Florentines

Makes 12

Ingredients
2oz [50g] caster sugar
2oz [50g] thinly flaked almonds
1 level tablespoonful plain flour
2oz [50g] plain chocolate, melted (optional)

1 tablespoon single cream
2oz [50g] mixed chopped glace
   cherries, angelica and candied peel
1 1/2oz [40g] butter

Method
Place sugar, almonds, flour, butter, single cream and the mixed fruits into a small saucepan, stir over a gentle heat until well mixed. Do not overheat, cool, then chill until firm. Put rounded teaspoons of the mixture onto well greased non-stick baking sheets or baking sheets lined with non-stick paper. Flatten each heap a little, to help it bake into a round shape. Bake just above centre of oven Mark 4/350°F/180°C for 10 minutes, or until just set and golden brown. Allow to cool for 1 to 2 minutes, then lift carefully off the sheet with a knife. When the Florentines are cold and crisp, brush the base of each with melted chocolate (if using).

• • • • • • • • •

20. Gypsy Creams

Ingredients

3oz [85g] margarine
6oz [175g] self-raising flour
2oz [50g] sugar
2 tablespoons milk

3 level tablespoons 3oz [85g]
   Golden Syrup
1 level tablespoon cocoa powder
2oz [50g] rolled oats

Ingredients for the Chocolate Cream

2oz [50g] margarine
3 level tablespoons cocoa

5oz [150g] sifted icing sugar
1 to 2 tablespoons evaporated or
   creamy milk

Method

Melt the margarine and syrup in a saucepan, stir in the sifted flour and cocoa, then mix in the sugar and rolled oats. Stir in the milk. Form into 32 balls, and place on greased baking sheets. Flatten with a fork dipped in hot water. Bake towards top of the oven at Mark 3/325°F/170°C for about 20 minutes. Cool before removing from the sheets. When cold, sandwich in pairs with chocolate cream, which is made by mixing all the ingredients together until creamy.

● ● ● ● ● ● ● ● ●

Bread and Buns

1. Afternoon Tea Buns
2. Date Loaf
3. French Bread
4. Fruit and Malt Loaf
5. Old Fashioned Spice Bread
6. Water Bread
7. Wholemeal Bread
8. Yeast Cake
9. Yorkshire Teacakes

Bread and Buns

1. Afternoon Tea Buns

Ingredients
1/2pt [300ml] milk
2oz [50g] butter or margarine
1 egg
1oz [25g] yeast

2oz [50g] sugar
2oz [50g] sultanas or currants
1lb [450g] flour
pinch of salt

Method
Warm the milk, and melt the butter in it, then add the beaten egg. Beat the yeast and sugar together until it creams. Mix with the dried fruit, flour and salt to a light dough. Put to rise, when risen make into small tea buns and allow to rise again. Bake in a hot oven for 20 minutes (Mark 6/400°F/200°C). When cooled, brush over with thin white icing. Makes about 28 buns.

2. Date Loaf

Ingredients
1lb [450g] dates
3/4pt [450ml] hot water
1 teaspoon bicarbonate soda
2oz [50g] margarine

2 eggs
6oz [175g] sugar
3/4lb [350g] flour
2 teaspoons baking powder

Method
Put into a bowl, the dates cut up small, water, soda and margarine. Let these melt together. Add the well beaten eggs, sugar, flour and baking powder. Mix well, put into two greased 2lb tins and bake in a moderate oven Mark 3/325°F/170°C for 1 hour.

3. French Bread

Ingredients

³/₄oz [21g] yeast
¹/₈pt [75ml] warm water
1 teaspoon sugar
2oz [50g] margarine

1lb [450g] flour
1 teaspoon salt
warm milk to mix

Method

Place yeast, water and sugar in warm place to rise. Rub margarine into flour in a warm bowl, pour yeast into centre, put salt round. Add sufficient warm milk and knead to a light dough. Leave 1 hour to rise. Roll out lightly and cut into rounds. Place on greased tins and let rise again for 20 minutes. Bake in preheated oven at Mark 7/425°F/220°C.

• • • • • • • • •

4. Fruit and Malt Loaf

Ingredients

¹/₂lb [225g] self-raising flour
¹/₄ teaspoon bicarbonate soda
³/₄ tablespoon brown sugar
3oz [75g] sultanas or currants

1 teaspoon salt
2 tablespoons syrup
1¹/₂ tablespoons extract of malt
¹/₄pt [150ml] milk

Method

Sieve the dry ingredients together, melt syrup and malt over a low heat in a pan, mix with the milk and pour over the dry ingredients. Bake in well greased loaf tin for 1 hour. Mark 4/350°F/180°C.

• • • • • • • • •

5.   Old Fashioned Spice Bread

Ingredients

1 1/2lb [675g] plain flour
little salt
2 teaspoons baking powder
1/2lb [225g] lard or butter
1lb [450g] sugar
1lb [450g] currants

1/2lb [225g] small seeded raisins
nutmeg to taste
1oz [25g] yeast
Approximately 1/2pt warm water
3 eggs

Method

Put flour, salt and baking powder into a mixing bowl, rub in fat, add sugar, fruit and nutmeg. Cream yeast with a little sugar and add a little warm milk. Beat the eggs thoroughly and add to the dry ingredients. Add the yeast and enough warm milk to make a not too soft mixture. Set to rise in 2 greased bread tins for 1 hour. Bake in a moderate oven for 2 hours. Mark 4/350°F/180°C.

• • • • • • • • •

6.   Water Bread

Running short of bread?

This recipe was used by the linen weavers of Yorkshire, about a century ago, as it was quicker than baking bread loaves. Sometimes toasted on both sides, split and buttered. In the old days a griddle or Yorkshire 'Bakeston' would have been used for baking.

Ingredients

1lb [450g] plain flour
2 small teaspoons baking powder

1/2 teaspoon salt
water to mix

Method

Mix the ingredients with water to make a firm dough. Roll out into flat cakes and place on a greased baking sheet. Allow to set for 5 minutes. Then bake in hot oven Mark 7/425°F/220°C for 20 to 30 minutes. This is very good, split and buttered while warm, or heat a little knob of butter with cheese slices as filling for sandwiches.

• • • • • • • • •

7.   Wholemeal Bread

Ingredients

3lb [1.35kg] 100% wheatmeal flour
3 teaspoons salt
2oz [50g] lard
1oz [25g] yeast

1 dessertspoon sugar
about 11oz [310g] warm water to
    each pound of flour

Method

Rub lard into the salt and flour. Leave to get warm. Cream the yeast with the sugar, add half of the water. Leave to sponge. When yeast has sponged and the flour is warm, stir yeast into the flour, making a stiff dough, and add the remainder of the warm water. Leave to rise for an hour or longer, knead well. Put into greased tins to rise until the dough has about doubled its height. Bake in a hot oven Mark 7/425°F/220°C for about 40 minutes, moving the tins to a cooler part of the oven after 20 minutes.

• • • • • • • • •

8.   Yeast Cake

2 greased 1lb [450g] loaf tins

Ingredients

1lb [450g] flour
1/4lb [115g] butter
1/4lb [115g] lard
1oz [25g] yeast
1lb [450g] brown sugar
a little milk

1/2lb [225g] currants
1/2lb [225] raisins or sultanas
1 teaspoon bicarbonate soda
nutmeg or spice optional
2 eggs

Method

Mix all the dry ingredients together. Rub in butter and lard. Put some milk to warm and let yeast rise in it for a few minutes, then mix with beaten eggs. Add to other ingredients. Mix well together and finally add the bicarbonate of soda in a little tepid milk, only half fill the cake tins. This quantity will make 2 cakes. Bake in a moderate oven Mark 4/350°F/180°C for about 3 hours. Do not turn out of tins until cold. This cake will keep for weeks.

• • • • • • • • •

9.   Yorkshire Teacakes

Ingredients

1lb [450g] flour
1 teaspoon salt
1oz [25g] lard
1oz [25g] yeast
1 teaspoon sugar

2oz [50g] currants or (currants,
    sultanas and peel mixed)
1oz [25g] sugar
$^1/_2$ to $^3/_4$pt [300 to 450ml] warm
    milk

Method

Sieve the flour and salt into a 2pt size earthenware bowl. Rub in the lard and put aside in a warm place, meanwhile, put the yeast and one teaspoon sugar into a cup to cream. Add fruit and sugar to warmed flour and with a wooden spoon make a well in the centre and pour in the yeast mixture and some of the milk at blood heat. Draw some of the flour into the centre and gradually add more warm milk and flour alternately to make a soft dough. Beat well, until smooth. Cover the basin with a clean cloth and leave in a warm place to rise to the top of the bowl for approximately one hour. Turn onto a floured board and knead together and divide into six portions, kneading one and rolling out flat. Place on a greased baking sheet. Leave to rise until height has doubled and spongy. Bake until golden brown for 10 to 15 minutes. Mark 6/400°F/200°C.

Scones

1. Apple Scones
2. Cheese Scones
3. Farmhouse Scones
4. Dropped Scones
5. Fat Rascals
6. Singin Hinnies

Scones

1.   Apple Scones

Ingredients

2oz [50g] lard
6oz [175g] flour
1oz [25g] sugar
1 teaspoon baking powder

1 large cooking apple (peeled and
   chopped)
1 egg
milk if necessary

Method

Sift flour and baking powder together, rub in lard. Add the apple finely chopped. Beat the egg in a very little milk and add to the dry ingredients to make a stiff elastic dough. Turn the dough onto lightly floured board, and divide into number of scones required. Shape and flatten by hand, about 1" thick and bake on greased baking sheet in moderate oven (Mark 6/400°F/200°C) for about half an hour. Dredge with sugar and serve hot buttered.

2.   Cheese Scones

Ingredients

1/2lb [225g] flour
1 1/2oz [40g] lard or margarine
good pinch of salt
1 egg

pinch dry mustard
1 1/2 teaspoons baking powder
2oz [50g] grated cheese
milk to mix

Method

Rub fat into flour and salt, add baking powder, mustard and grated cheese. Add well beaten egg and milk if needed to make it sufficiently moist for scones. Turn dough onto lightly floured surface, knead lightly, cut into rounds or triangles. Place on greased baking sheet, brush lightly with beaten egg or milk. Bake at Mark 6/400°F/200°C temperature for 10 to 12 minutes.

3. Farmhouse Scones

Ingredients

¹/₂lb [225g] plain flour
¹/₄ level teaspoon salt
I level tablespoon sugar
¹/₄pt [150ml] milk

3 level teaspoons baking powder
2oz [50g] lard or margarine
2oz [50g] currants or sultanas

Method

Sift the flour, salt and baking powder together. Rub in lard until mixture resembles breadcrumbs. Stir in sugar and currants (or sultanas). Stir in enough milk to make a dough that is soft but not sticky. Knead on a lightly floured surface to remove any large cracks, then roll out to ¹/₂ or ³/₄" thickness. Cut into rounds or triangles. Place on a baking sheet dusted with flour. Brush with milk and bake scones towards the top of the oven preset at Mark 8/450°F/230°C for 10 to 15 minutes. Made without the fruit, these scones are delicious with jam and cream.

• • • • • • • •

4. Dropped Scones

Ingredients

I egg
¹/₄lb [115g] sugar
I level tablespoon treacle

I level teaspoon bicarbonate soda
I level teaspoon cream of tartar
¹/₂lb [225g] plain flour

Method

Put egg, sugar and treacle in a basin and beat well. Add flour, other ingredients and milk, beating well until the mixture is the consistency of thick cream. Cook at once on a hot greased griddle by dropping the mixture from a spoon. Turn over when the mixture bubbles and cook the other side. The griddle should be hot enough to melt the greasing fat very quickly, but not hot enough to make it smoke. Makes 30 to 36 scones. N.B. These scones should be cooked on a griddle, but can be made quite successfully on a heavy based frying pan on top of stove.

• • • • • • • •

5.   Fat Rascals

A very old recipe! Another name given to fat rascals, on the Whitby moors, was turf cakes, where they were cooked over an open turf or peat fire on a griddle.

Ingredients
¹/₂lb [225g] self-raising flour   1oz [25g] sultanas
¹/₄lb [115g] lard   pinch of salt
3oz [85g] sugar   water or beaten egg
2oz [50g] currants

Method
Rub the lard into the flour and add the dry ingredients. Mix to a fairly soft dough with a little water or to make extra good use a little well beaten egg. Roll out to about ¹/₂" thickness and cut into rounds or triangles. Bake in a hot oven (Mark 5/450°F/230°C), for about 15 minutes or until nicely browned. Makes about 24 pieces.

·········

6.   Singin Hinnies

So called because of the noise they make when cooking!
Makes 16

Ingredients
³/₄lb [350g] self-raising flour   2oz [50g] currants
1 level teaspoon salt   2oz [50g] sugar
1oz [25g] lard   ¹/₂pt [300ml] milk
2oz [50g] ground rice   Griddle or heavy based frying pan

Method
Rub griddle or frying pan with a little extra lard and place it over a very low heat, to heat up. Put the flour and salt into a large bowl, rub in lard, until mixture is like breadcrumbs. Stir in the ground rice, currants and sugar. Make a well in the centre and add enough milk to give a soft, scone-like dough. Cut the dough in half, and on a floured surface, knead each piece until smooth. Shape into a ball, then pat or roll out into a 6" round. Cut each round into 8. Arrange the scones on a hot griddle and cook gently for about 10 minutes. Turn each scone over and cook for a further 10 minutes. Serve hot, split and buttered.

Pastries

1. Short Pastry
2. Short Pastry – Semi Sweet
3. Short Pastry – Rich and Sweet
4. Flaky Pastry
5. Puff Pastry
6. Choux Pastry – Use for Cream Buns and Eclairs

Pastries

1. Short Pastry

Ingredients

½lb [225g] flour
2oz [50g] lard
cold water to mix

pinch of salt
2oz [50g] margarine

Method

Sieve flour and salt. Rub fats in flour, until it resembles fine breadcrumbs. Mix with cold water to a firm dough.

2. Short Pastry – Semi Sweet for Tarts etc

Ingredients

½lb [225g] flour
1oz [25g] sugar
2oz [50g] margarine

¼ teaspoon salt
2oz [50g] lard
cold water (approximately 8
   teaspoons)

Method

Sieve flour and salt. Rub in fats until it resembles fine breadcrumbs. Add sugar. Mix with water to a firm dough.

3.   Short Pastry – Sweet and Rich

Ingredients

¹/₂lb [225g] flour
2oz [50g] lard
I egg, beaten

3oz [85g] margarine
3oz [85g] sugar

Method

Sieve flour. Rub in fats, until it resembles fine breadcrumbs. Mix in sugar. Add beaten egg, mix to smooth paste.

• • • • • • • • •

4.   Flaky Pastry

Ingredients

¹/₂lb [225g] plain flour
3oz [85g] lard
pinch cream of tartar

3oz [85g] margarine
squeeze lemon juice

Method

Sieve flour and cream of tartar. Blend fats and divide into four. Rub one part into flour, add lemon juice if used and bind with cold water. Roll out into long oblong, using another section of the divided fat, place it in small dabs over two thirds of the surface of the dough. Fold dough in three with plain piece in the centre. Seal the edges with a rolling pin and roll out. Repeat until all the fat is used up, and then roll and fold twice more. The pastry should be set aside in a cool place between each operation.

• • • • • • • • •

5.   Puff Pastry

Ingredients

1 lb [450g] plain flour   squeeze of lemon juice
1 lb [450g] butter

Method

Rub 2oz of the fat into the flour as for short crust pastry. Add the lemon juice and bind with cold water to make an elastic dough. Roll into a long oblong. Put the remainder of the butter in one piece into the centre of the oblong and fold the dough over it in three. Set aside in a cool place for at least 30 minutes. Seal and roll and refold pastry seven times, allowing it to cool between each rolling.

• • • • • • • • •

6.   Choux Pastry

Ingredients

1/2pt [300ml] water   1/2oz [15g] sugar
3oz [85g] butter   3 eggs
5oz [150g] flour

Method

Heat the water and butter in a pan and when boiling add the sifted flour, stir briskly while still heating, until the paste is smooth and leaves the sides of the saucepan. Add the sugar, allow to cool and then beat in the eggs a little at a time. Use for cream buns and eclairs.

• • • • • • • • •

Cakes

1. Almond and Cherry Cake
2. Angel Cake
3. Apricot and Walnut Cake
4. Birthday Cake
5. Butterscotch Cake
6. Carrot Cake
7. Coconut Cake
8. Coffee Cake
9. Crusty Lemon Butter Cake
10. Cut and Come Again Cake
11. Dream Cake
12. Dundee Cake
13. Fudge Brownies
14. Mocha Cake
15. Rich Chocolate Cake
16. Sly Cake
17. Spicy Rock Buns
18. Sponge Cake
19. Yorkshire Curd Tarts
20. Family Christmas Cake
21. Almond Paste
22. Royal Icing

Cakes

1.   Almond and Cherry Cake

Ingredients

$^1/_4$lb [115g] butter
$^1/_4$lb [115g] sugar
2 eggs
salt
7oz [200g] flour

1 teaspoon baking powder
2oz [50g] ground almonds
2oz [50g] glace cherries
little milk to mix

Method

Cream the butter and sugar. Beat eggs with a pinch of salt and add gradually to the creamed mixture. Sieve flour and baking powder and add with the almonds gradually, also add cherries cut in half and lightly floured. Add milk as required to make a fairly moist mixture. Put into well greased 8" tin and bake in moderate to slow oven Mark 5/375°F/190°C for 1$^1/_4$ hours, perhaps longer. Can be covered with white icing and decorated with cherries and almonds when cold.

2.   Angel Cake

Ingredients

$^1/_4$lb [115g] butter
$^1/_4$lb [115g] sugar
6oz [175g] cornflour
Tin 5$^1/_2$" by 3$^1/_2$"

$^1/_2$ teaspoon baking powder
whites of 3 eggs
a few drops almond essence

Method

Beat butter and sugar to a cream. Sift cornflour with the baking powder, stir lightly into the creamed mixture, alternately with the stiffly whisked egg whites. Transfer to tin lined with greased paper and bake for 65 minutes at Mark 4/350°F/180°C.

3.   Apricot and Walnut Cake

Ingredients

¹/₂lb [225g] dried apricots
2oz [50g] walnuts
¹/₂lb [225g] plain flour
4 level teaspoons baking powder
¹/₂lb [225g] wholewheat flour
2lb loaf tin

6oz [175g] butter
¹/₂lb [225g] soft brown sugar
2 eggs
¹/₄pt [150ml] plus 2 tablespoons
   milk

For the Topping

2 dessertspoons clear honey
1oz [25g] caster sugar

1oz [25g] butter
1oz [25g] chopped walnuts

Method

Butter the tin and line the base with buttered greaseproof paper and cut to fit. Chop the apricots and walnuts. Sift the plain flour and baking powder into a mixing bowl, then mix in the wholewheat flour. Rub in the butter, then mix in the soft brown sugar, chopped apricots and walnuts. Beat the eggs with the milk, stir into the dry ingredients. Turn mixture into the tin and smooth over the surface. Bake in moderate oven for 1 hour Mark 4/180°F/350°F, then reduce the heat to Mark 3/325°F/170°C for a further 1 hour, 20 minutes before loaf is ready, melt together the ingredients for topping, and coat the top of the loaf. Return to oven for 20 minutes and when cooked, leave to cool slightly before turning out onto wire rack. To serve, spread thick slices with butter.

· · · · · · · · ·

4.   Birthday Cake

Ingredients

¹/₄lb [115g] butter
¹/₄lb [115g] sugar
2 eggs
¹/₄lb [115g] flour

2oz [50g] ground almonds
³/₄lb [350g] currants
2 tablespoons brandy
3oz [85g] mixed peel

Method

Beat butter and sugar to a cream, add each egg separately and beat until the mixture is stiff and uniform. Stir in the flour, ground almonds, fruit and brandy. Transfer to the tin, well lined with greased paper and bake for 2 hours at Mark 2/300°F/150°C. The cake should be kept for 2 to 3 weeks before being decorated.

5. Butterscotch Cake

Ingredients

¹/₄lb [115g] butter
¹/₄lb [115g] soft brown sugar
2 eggs, separated
1 tablespoon syrup
1 teaspoon vanilla essence

3floz milk
¹/₄lb [115g] plain flour
2oz [50g] cornflour
2 level teaspoons baking powder
¹/₂ level teaspoon cinnamon

Method

Grease and line two 7" sandwich tins. Cream butter and sugar together, add egg yolks, syrup, vanilla and milk and beat well. Sieve the dry ingredients together and fold into the creamed mixture. Whisk egg whites until stiff and fold in. Turn into prepared tins and bake at Mark 5/375°F/190°C for 20 to 25 minutes. When cool sandwich together with butter icing and sprinkle icing sugar on the top. (See Icings).

• • • • • • • • •

6. Carrot Cake

Ingredients

¹/₄lb [115g] butter or margarine
¹/₄lb [115g] caster sugar
2 large eggs
¹/₂lb [225g] carrots peeled and
  coarsely grated

¹/₄lb [115g] self-raising flour
7" by 7" shallow cake tin (based
  lined and greased)
finely grated rind of 1 lemon

Method

Cream the butter or margarine until soft, then add the sugar and beat until light and fluffy. Add the eggs, one at a time, beating well at each addition. Beat in the lemon rind with a metal spoon, fold in carrot and then flour. Spread the mixture evenly over the tin, then bake just above centre oven at Mark 4/350°F/180°C for 30 to 35 minutes or until firm and springy to the touch. When cold, cut into fingers.

• • • • • • • • •

7.   Coconut Cake

Ingredients

1/2lb [225g] margarine
6oz [175g] caster sugar
3 large eggs
6oz [175g] self-raising flour

2oz [50g] desiccated coconut
1 tablespoon milk
1 large orange
6oz [175g] sifted icing sugar

Method

Grease two 7 1/2" sandwich tins. Cream 6oz margarine with the caster sugar. Beat eggs and gradually add to creamed mixture, beating all the time. Sift the flour and fold into the mixture, with a metal spoon. Soak 1oz coconut in the milk, then fold into the mixture. Pour into prepared tins and bake in centre of oven at Mark 3/325°F/170°C for 25 to 30 minutes or until golden brown and firm to touch. Turn out to cool. Squeeze the juice from orange and soak the rest of the coconut in this, cream the remaining 2oz margarine with icing sugar. Beat in coconut mixture. Sandwich the cakes with half of this and spread the rest on top. Decorate with pieces of orange with rind left on.

· · · · · · · · ·

8.   Coffee Cake

Delicious eaten with coffee.

Ingredients

6oz [175g] sugar
1 egg
6oz [175g] flour
1/4 teaspoon salt

2oz [50g] margarine
4 tablespoons milk
1 teaspoon baking powder

Streusel Topping

1/4lb [115g] brown sugar
1/2oz [15g] flour
Mix together

1oz [25g] melted butter
1/2 cup chopped nuts
1 teaspoon cinnamon

Method

Cream the sugar and margarine together and add the beaten egg and milk, stir the flour, baking powder and salt into the mixture. Put half this mixture into a greased and floured square 9" tin, sprinkle with half of the streusel topping. Spread on the rest of the cake mixture and sprinkle with the remaining topping. Bake for 25 to 35 minutes at Mark 5/375°F/190°C.

· · · · · · · · ·

9. Crusty Lemon Butter Cake

Ingredients
6oz [175g] butter
6oz [175g] caster sugar

2 eggs
10oz [300g] self-raising flour

For the Crusty Top
Juice of 1 lemon
A straight sided tin 14" by 9"

about another 1/4lb [115g] caster
sugar

Method
Butter the tin, put butter into a mixing bowl and cut into small pieces, stand the bowl in a warm place until the butter begins to melt and when it is soft, stir in the sugar. Beat the eggs together and stir them into the mixture with the flour. Turn the mixture into the prepared tin and smooth over the surface. Bake in a moderate oven Mark 4/350°F/180°C, for about 40 minutes when the surface should be soft, though set and lightly golden. Take it out of the oven, and while it is still hot, mix enough caster sugar with the lemon juice to make a thin paste. Spread this quickly over the surface, the lemon juice sinks in to the surface, leaving the top crispy when cold.

• • • • • • • • •

10. Cut and Come Again Cake

Ingredients
6oz [175g] sugar
6oz [175g] margarine
2 eggs
almond essence
milk

1/2lb [225g] plain flour
2 teaspoons baking powder
5 to 6oz [150 to 175g] mixed dried
fruit

Method
Cream the sugar and margarine, then add the well beaten eggs, fold in the sieved flour and baking powder and dried fruits and 2 to 3 tablespoons milk to make a soft dropping consistency. Flavouring may be added if desired. Line the bottom of a greased 9" cake tin with greased paper. Put in the mixture, smooth the top and bake in a moderate oven Mark 4/350°F/180°C for about 1 1/4 hours.

• • • • • • • • •

11.   Dream Cake

This cake consists of a cherry, nut and meringue mixture which is baked on top of a shortbread crust in a deep swiss roll tin about 10" by 12".

The Crust
1/4lb [115g] butter or margarine	1/2lb [225g] sifted plain flour
2 tablespoons icing sugar	pinch of salt

Method
Rub fat into dry ingredients until consistency of breadcrumbs is reached. Spread evenly in the greased tin. Press down lightly.

Topping
2 eggs	2oz [50g] sifted flour
1/2lb [225g] caster sugar	pinch of salt
1 teaspoon baking powder	1 teaspoon vanilla essence
3oz [85g] chopped walnuts	2oz [50g] chopped cherries
2oz [50g] desiccated coconut	

Method
Beat eggs and sugar together well. Stir in other ingredients. Pour the mixture on top of lower crust, bake in a slow oven Mark 4/350°F/180°C 30 to 50 minutes until meringue top is light golden colour and firm to the touch. This cake keeps well for a long time, though your family will not give you a chance to find out exactly how long!!!

· · · · · · · · ·

12.   Dundee Cake

Ingredients
1/2lb [225g] butter	2oz [50g] cherries
1/2lb [225g] sugar	1/4lb [115g] blanched almonds
10oz [275g] flour	pinch of salt
5 eggs	almond essence
1/2lb [225g] currants	grated orange rind
1/2lb [225g] sultanas	1/8 teaspoon bicarbonate soda,
1/4lb [115g] candied peel	dissolved in a little milk

Method

Beat the butter and sugar to a cream. Beat the eggs. Add gradually half of the eggs to the creamed butter and sugar, beating well, until smooth and thick. Stir in half the flour, then add the remainder of the eggs gradually, beating well. Add the fruit, peel, half of the chopped almonds and the rest of the flour. Mix together, adding the soda dissolved in the milk. Turn into 8" cake tin greased and lined with greased paper. Sprinkle the remainder of the almonds on top and bake for $3^1/2$ hours at Mark 2/300°F/150°C.

• • • • • • • •

13.   Fudge Brownies

A popular American recipe. Brownies are really mouthwatering.

Ingredients for Cake

$^1/4$lb [115g] butter or margarine	2oz [50g] plain flour
$^1/2$lb [225g] dark soft brown sugar	1oz [25g] cocoa
2 eggs	$^1/2$ level teaspoon baking powder
1 teaspoon vanilla essence	1 tablespoon milk
$^1/4$lb [115g] chopped walnuts	

Topping

3oz [85g] plain chocolate	1 tablespoon boiling water
2 tablespoons milk	6oz [175g] icing sugar
1oz [25g] butter or margarine	1 teaspoon instant coffee

Method for Cake

Preheat oven Mark 4/350°F/180°C. Grease 12" by 8" by 2" tin and line base with greased, greaseproof paper, cream fat and sugar together until light and fluffy. Beat in the eggs one at a time, stir in the vanilla essence. Sift flour, cocoa and baking powder together and fold into creamed mixture with walnuts and milk. Pour into the tin and level the top. Bake in centre of moderate oven for 30 to 35 minutes. Turn out and leave to cool on a wire rack.

To make Topping

Melt chocolate in a bowl over a saucepan of hot, not boiling water. Add milk, fat and coffee dissolved in a tablespoon of boiling water, stir in icing sugar and beat until smooth. Spread over cooled cake mixture and leave to set. Cut into 15 squares.

• • • • • • • •

14.   Mocha Cake

Ingredients

$^1/_4$lb [115g] butter
$^1/_4$lb [115g] caster sugar
2 eggs
$^1/_4$lb [115g] flour
Size of tin 5$^1/_2$" by 3"

$^1/_4$ teaspoon baking powder
a little flavouring
coffee icing
butter icing

Method

Beat the sugar and butter to a cream, add each egg separately and beat well, lightly fold in the flour and baking powder, add flavouring. Butter a plain tin, dust with caster sugar and flour, pour in the mixture and bake for 1$^1/_4$ hours at Mark 3/325°F/160°C. When cold, cover with coffee icing and decorate with butter icing (see section for icing).

· · · · · · · · ·

15.   Rich Chocolate Cake

Ingredients

3oz [85g] butter
3oz [85g] sugar
3oz [85g] flour
3 eggs

3oz [85g] chocolate powder
vanilla essence
1 level teaspoon baking powder

Method

Cream butter and sugar, add flour and beaten eggs alternately (keeping back 1 egg white). Add chocolate powder, vanilla and baking powder, and last of all the stiffly beaten egg white, bake in two 8" sandwich tins or in a 2" deep sponge tin (well greased) for 25 to 35 minutes at Mark 6/375°F/190°C.

Filling

1oz [25g] chocolate powder
1 tablespoon cream

2oz [50g] butter

Method

Beat to a cream.

Icing

2oz [50g] milk chocolate bar
1 small piece butter

3oz [85g] icing sugar
1 dessertspoon warm water

Method

Melt chocolate on a plate over hot water, mix in butter, icing sugar and water. Beat well and spread on cake.

16.   Sly Cake

Ingredients

¹/₂lb [225g] flour
¹/₄lb [115g] sugar
¹/₄lb [115g] margarine

1 teaspoon baking powder
1 egg
little jam for filling

Method

Rub margarine into flour and baking powder until like breadcrumbs. Mix in sugar, bind with beaten egg. Knead lightly and divide into two parts. Roll out thinly and put on a greased baking sheet, with a thin layer of jam between the two pieces. Brush with milk and sprinkle a little sugar on top. Bake in a moderate oven for about 20 to 25 minutes. Mark 6/400°F/200°C.

• • • • • • • • •

17.   Spicy Rock Buns

Makes 12 to 16 Buns

Ingredients

³/₄lb [350g] plain flour
2 teaspoons baking powder
¹/₂ teaspoon ground nutmeg
1 teaspoon mixed spice
6oz [175g] caster sugar
pinch of salt

6oz [175g] butter or margarine
¹/₄lb [115g] currants
3oz [85g] mixed peel
1 egg, beaten
1 to 2 tablespoons milk

Method

Grease 2 baking sheets, sieve the dry ingredients into a bowl. Rub in the butter with fingertips until it resembles fine breadcrumbs and stir in the currants and mixed peel. Add the egg and enough liquid to form a crumbly dough. Spoon large teaspoons onto the baking sheet and cook for about 20 to 25 minutes at Mark 6/400°F/200°C until firm and golden. Leave to cool on a wire rack.

• • • • • • • • •

18.   Sponge Cake

Ingredients

3 eggs separated
1/4lb [115g] flour

5oz [150g] caster sugar (warmed)
8" deep cake tin, greased and lined
   with greaseproof paper

Method

Put the whites of eggs into a bowl and whisk until stiff, add sugar and yolks of eggs and whisk vigorously for 5 minutes. Fold in flour a little at a time and bake at Mark 5/375°F/190°C in prepared tin for 30 minutes or until set. To serve, split cake in two, spread with jam and cream and dust top with icing sugar.

• • • • • • • •

19.   Yorkshire Curd Tarts

A Yorkshire speciality
Makes 6 to 8

Ingredients

1/2lb [225g] plain flour
pinch of salt
1/2lb [225g] butter
5oz [150g] caster sugar
1 egg yolk
2 to 3 tablespoons cold water

1/2lb [225g] curd cheese
1 egg
2oz [50g] sultanas
pinch of mixed spice
1 tablespoon sieved icing sugar to
   dust

Method

Place the flour and salt into a bowl. Rub in 4oz butter until it resembles fine breadcrumbs. Stir in 1 tablespoon caster sugar and mix in the egg yolk and enough water to form a soft dough. Knead lightly until smooth, then roll out on a floured surface. Cut around a saucer and use to line 6 to 8 large Yorkshire pudding tins, greased, or you can use saucers. To make filling, cream the remaining butter and caster sugar until light, gradually beat in the cheese, egg, sultanas and spice. Spoon the mixture into the prepared tins or saucers. Cook for 25 to 30 minutes at Mark 6/400°F/200°C. Lightly dust with sieved icing sugar. Serve warm or cold with cream.

• • • • • • • •

20. Family Christmas Cake

Ingredients for Cake

10oz [275g] plain flour
1/2 level teaspoon salt
1/2 level teaspoon mixed spice
1/2 level teaspoon nutmeg
1/2lb [225g] butter
1/2lb [225g] dark soft brown sugar
4 large eggs
3/4lb [350g] stoned raisins (chopped)

1/2lb [225g] currants
1/2lb [225g] sultanas
2oz [50g] glace cherries, quartered
2oz [50g] blanched almonds,
    chopped
1 tablespoon black treacle
grated rind and juice of 1 orange
2 tablespoons of brandy

Almond Icing

3/4lb [350g] ground almonds
6oz [175g] icing sugar, sieved
6oz [175g] caster sugar
4 egg yolks

1 teaspoon almond essence
4 tablespoons apricot jam (warmed
    and sieved)

Royal Icing

4 egg whites
about 2lbs [900g] icing sugar, sieved

juice of 1 lemon
3 teaspoons glycerine

Method for Cake

1. Grease a 9" round tin and line with double thickness of greaseproof paper.
2. Sift together flour, salt and spices.
3. Beat butter and sugar together until pale and creamy.
4. Add beaten egg a little at a time, beating well after each addition.
5. Fold in 2 tablespoons of flour mixture with the last amount of egg.
6. Fold in remaining flour alternately with fruit.
7. Add all remaining ingredients, except brandy.
8. Mix well, turn into prepared tin, smooth top.
9. Bake Gas Mark 2/300°F/150°C, for 1 1/2 hours.
10. Reduce oven temperature to Mark 1/275°F/140°C bake further 2 hours, or until skewer inserted in centre comes out clean.
11. Cool in tin for 10 minutes, then turn out onto a wire rack and leave to finish cooling.
12. When almost cold, make holes with a fine skewer over top of cake, pour over brandy.
13. When completely cold, wrap in foil and store in tin.

Almond Paste

14. Put all ingredients in a bowl.
15. Mix with wooden spoon until bound together, then knead by hand until a smooth paste is formed.
16. Brush cake with jam.
17. Roll out one third paste to a circle for the top. Use the remainder for 2 strips to go round side of cake. Press firmly onto cake.
18. Leave for 3 days before icing.

Royal Icing

19. Whisk egg whites in bowl until light and frothy.
20. Beat in icing sugar a tablespoon at a time.
21. Add lemon juice and glycerine after half of sugar.
22. Continue to add icing sugar, beating well, until icing forms fairly stiff peaks.
23. Cover with foil and leave at least 2 hours.
24. Spread all over cake evenly, rough icing up in peaks with a palette knife, or smooth and pipe.
25. Decorate with ribbons, candles, or Christmas decorations. Stand cake on 11" round silver cake board.

Notes

Make cake before end of November, almond paste 10 days before Christmas, and ice a couple of days beforehand. The 2lb icing sugar is on the generous side to allow for icing for piping, so if you are just rough icing the cake, you could use only 1 1/2lb sugar and 3 egg whites.

Icing for Cakes

1. Almond Paste
2. Economical Almond Paste
3. Water or Glace Icing
4. Orange Glace Icing
5. Coffee Glace Icing
6. Chocolate Glace Icing
7. Orange and Honey Cream
8. Chocolate Butter Icing
9. Lemon Curd Cream
10. Brandy or Rum Butter

Flavourings for Butter Cream Icing

1. Chocolate Butter Cream Icing
2. Peppermint Butter Cream Icing
3. Orange Butter Cream Icing
4. Coffee Butter Cream Icing
5. Lemon Butter Cream Icing
6. Vanilla Cream
7. Lemon Curd

Icing for Cakes

1. Almond Paste

Ingredients

6oz [175g] caster sugar
1 egg or 3 yolks
1 teaspoon vanilla essence

6oz [175g] sieved icing sugar
3/4lb [350g] ground almonds
juice of half lemon

Method

Mix ground almonds and sugars. Beat the egg or 3 yolks, and add the flavourings, pour onto the dry ingredients. Mix to a pliable, but not sticky paste with a fork. If necessary, add more lemon juice or icing sugar to bring to the correct consistency.

2. Economical Almond Paste

Ingredients

1/4lb [115g] semolina
2oz [50g] margarine
1 1/2 teaspoons almond essence

2 tablespoons water
1/4lb [115g] granulated sugar

Method

Melt the margarine in the water in a saucepan, add semolina, stir over gentle heat for 1 minute. Stir in sugar, over gentle heat, remove saucepan from the heat and stir in the essence. Cool until stiff enough to roll out. The amount of paste made from this recipe is equivalent to 6oz ground almonds (See recipe for almond paste).

3. Water or Glace Icing

Ingredients

colouring
1/2lb [225g] sieved icing sugar

2 to 2 1/2 tablespoons warm water
good squeeze lemon juice

Method

Put sugar into a saucepan, add lemon juice. Add water cautiously and mix to a coating consistency. Colour to taste. Beat well, stir over gentle heat for 1 minute.

• • • • • • • • •

4. Orange Glace Icing

Make as for water or glace icing, using strained orange juice instead of water.

• • • • • • • • •

5. Coffee Glace Icing

Make as water icing, but use half coffee essence and half water for mixing.

• • • • • • • • •

6. Chocolate Glace Icing

Ingredients

1/4lb [115g] plain chocolate
6oz [175g] sieved icing sugar

small knob of butter
2 to 2 1/2 tablespoons warm water

Method

Cut the chocolate into small pieces with a knife, put it and the butter into a saucepan with 1 1/2 tablespoons of warm water. Stir over gentle heat to a smooth cream. Cool until lukewarm, add the sugar by degrees, beating thoroughly and adding a little water, if required, to bring to a coating consistency. Beat again over a gentle heat, test the consistency, then pour over the cake.

• • • • • • • • •

7. Orange and Honey Cream

Ingredients

2oz [50g] butter
1 tablespoon honey (medium stiff)
3oz [85g] sieved icing sugar

1 level teaspoon finely grated orange rind

Method

Beat the fat until soft, add the sugar and beat to a cream, stir in the honey and grated orange rind gradually and beat again.

• • • • • • • • •

8. Chocolate Butter Icing

Ingredients

1/2lb [225g] sieved icing sugar
1/4lb [115g] butter
5oz [150g] plain chocolate

vanilla essence
1/8pt [75ml] water

Method

Shred chocolate finely with a knife, place in a small saucepan with the water. Stir over gentle heat until smooth, then cool. Beat the fat until soft, beat in the sugar gradually, then melted chocolate and essence. Use at once. If the icing becomes too firm, beat over gentle heat.

• • • • • • • • •

9. Lemon Curd Cream

Ingredients

2oz [50g] butter
1 1/2 tablespoons lemon curd

3oz [85g] sieved icing sugar

Method

Beat the fat until soft, add the sugar and beat to a cream. Stir in the lemon curd gradually and beat again.

• • • • • • • • •

10.   Brandy or Rum Butter

Ingredients

3oz [85g] sugar

nutmeg

1/4lb [115g] fresh butter

rum or brandy to taste

Method

Beat the butter and sugar to a cream and add brandy or rum to taste. Pile in a dish, and lightly dredge with powdered nutmeg.

Flavourings for Butter Cream Icing

1.   Chocolate Butter Cream Icing

Add 1oz [25g] grated plain chocolate dissolved in the hot milk.

• • • • • • • • •

2.   Peppermint Butter Cream Icing

Delicious for chocolate cake

Add 2 or 3 drops of peppermint essence and 2 or 3 drops of green colouring.

• • • • • • • • •

3.   Orange Butter Cream Icing

Add $1/2$ teaspoon finely grated orange rind and 2 or 3 drops of orange colouring.

• • • • • • • • •

4.   Coffee Butter Cream Icing

Add 1 teaspoon coffee extract, dissolved in the hot milk.

• • • • • • • • •

5.   Lemon Butter Cream Icing

Add 1 teaspoon lemon curd.

• • • • • • • • •

6. Vanilla Cream

Ingredients

2oz [50g] butter or margarine
2oz [50g] icing or caster sugar
1/4pt [150ml] milk

1 rounded teaspoon cornflour
1/4 teaspoon vanilla essence

Method

Blend the cornflour with milk, boil until thick, stirring all the time. Leave until cold with a piece of wet paper over the surface to prevent a skin forming. Cream the fat and sugar until very soft, the same consistency as the cornflour sauce. Add the latter a spoonful at a time, beating well after each addition. Beat in essence and use as required.

• • • • • • • • •

7. Lemon Curd

Ingredients

6oz [175g] butter
4 eggs

1lb [450g] loaf sugar
3 lemons

Method

Wipe lemons and grate rinds, melt butter in a double saucepan, add sugar, lemon juice and grated rinds and dissolve. Add the beaten eggs and stir constantly until it thickens. Pour into pots. Cover as for jam.

Salads

1. Green Salads
2. Salads made from Cooked Vegetables
3. Fish or Meat Salads
4. Fruit Salads
5. Typical Fruit Salad
6. Vegetarian Salads

Salad Dressing

1. Salad Cream
2. Salad Cream for Bottling
3. French Dressing
4. Hurry Up Mayonnaise
5. Mayonnaise

Salads

Salads can be divided into four kinds:

1. Green salads made from lettuces, watercress, cucumber, tomatoes, etc.
2. Salads made from cooked vegetables, e.g. potatoes, beetroot, etc.
3. Fish or meat, made from cooked fish, or meat and green salad.
4. Fruit.

Salads should always be made from young, sound vegetables or fruit. General preparations for

1. Green Salads

1. Wash the vegetables well, in cold water, not salt water. N.B. Salt water will make lettuce etc., limp.
2. Dry in a clean cloth, being careful not to bruise the leaves.
3. Keep the best parts of the vegetables to decorate the top of the salad.
4. If salad is made some time before using, tear the lettuce in small pieces with the fingers, but otherwise they can be cut with a sharp knife. This improves the appearance of the salad.
5. Salad dressing can be poured over, or served separately.

2. Salads Made from Cooked Vegetables

1. The vegetables should be firm and not at all mashed.
2. Cut into neat pieces and arrange attractively.
3. Pour over a salad dressing and decorate with hard boiled egg.

3. Fish or Meat Salads

1. Divide the meat into neat portions, removing any bones.
2. Arrange green salad and the meat or fish in layers.
3. Coat each layer of fish or meat with a thick salad dressing.

•••••••••

4. Fruit Salads

1. Cut the fruits into neat slices.
2. Remove any tough skin or stones.
3. Keep the best coloured and shaped pieces of fruit to decorate the top of the salad.
4. Fruit salad should be made several hours before serving.

•••••••••

5. A Typical Fruit Salad

Ingredients

sugar   any fresh fruit available
tin of pineapple   bananas
orange juice   apples
lemon juice   nuts, almonds for preference

Method

Boil with the sugar, the juices from the pineapple, the orange and the lemon. Peel and slice the bananas and apples and mix with the other fruits and nuts. Pour the boiling juice over the fruits and leave until quite cold before serving. When fresh fruit is difficult to obtain, prunes, peaches and other dried fruits can be substituted. Soak and stew the dried fruit before mixing with other fruits.

•••••••••

6.   Vegetarian Salads

1. Ingredients

cabbage   salad dressing
salt and pepper   walnuts

Method
Slice finely the heart of a cabbage, sprinkle with salt and pepper and coat with custard salad dressing or mayonnaise (see chapter for sauces etc., under Miscellaneous). Chop the walnuts and sprinkle them thickly over the cabbage.

2. Ingredients

bananas   1/4pt [150ml] milk
lettuce   1 egg
walnuts   salt, pepper, made mustard
beetroot   sugar
1/2oz [15g] butter   lemon juice
1/2oz [15g] flour

Method
To prepare the dressing, melt butter in saucepan, then add the flour and heat for a minute. Pour in the milk, stir and boil to make a smooth sauce. Remove from heat and cool by beating. Add the yolk of the egg and beat well. Cook gently until thick. Turn off heat and add salt, pepper and mustard, sugar and lemon juice to taste. Cool, whisk stiffly the egg white and fold into the sauce. Peel and scrape the bananas. If small leave whole, but if large, cut into halves or quarters. Wash and dry lettuce and shred or tear up. Grate the beetroot if raw or cut into cubes if cooked. Chop the walnuts and arrange on a bed of lettuce on individual plates. Coat the bananas with the dressing and place them on the lettuce. Sprinkle with the chopped walnuts and decorate with the beetroot.

3. Ingredients

grated raw carrot   pine kernels
grated raw turnip   salt and pepper
watercress   cream cheese

Method
Wash, peel and grate the carrot and turnip. Wash the watercress. Arrange the whole tastefully together. Sprinkle with pine kernels and serve with cream cheese and wholemeal bread.

4. Ingredients

cold, boiled or steamed potatoes

grated cheese

mayonnaise

parsley

Method

Slice the cold potatoes or cut into cubes, arrange in a dish with layers of grated cheese and mayonnaise. Decorate with chopped parsley.

Salad Dressings

1.   Salad Cream

Ingredients

1 small teaspoon mustard
5 teaspoons sugar
dash of pepper and salt to taste

5 tablespoons cream
5 tablespoons vinegar

Method

Mix dry ingredients together. Add cream, a little at a time, then add the vinegar.
Sufficient to serve 6 to 7 persons.

2.   Salad Cream for Bottling

Ingredients

2 teaspoons cornflour
1 teaspoon mustard
1 tablespoon sugar
^{1}/$_2$pt [300ml] milk
^{1}/$_4$pt [150ml] vinegar

pepper and salt
2 egg yolks
2 tablespoons salad oil (or melted
    butter)

Method

Mix all the dry ingredients, add milk to eggs, yolks only and add to the mixture, then
gradually add the oil and vinegar. Cook in a double saucepan or milk pan until it
thickens. Bottle.

3. French Dressing

Ingredients
pinch of salt
pinch of sugar
pinch of mustard
pinch of pepper

good squeeze lemon juice
1 tablespoon olive oil
2 tablespoons tarragon vinegar

Method
Dissolve the dry ingredients in vinegar with the lemon juice. Lastly add the oil slowly to blend well.

· · · · · · · · ·

4. 'Hurry Up' Mayonnaise

Ingredients
2 tablespoons vinegar
little paprika
$1/2$ teaspoon salt
1 teaspoon prepared mustard

$1/2$ teaspoon sugar
1 egg yolk
$1/4$ teaspoon pepper
salad oil

Method
Put egg yolk in a deep bowl. Heat the other ingredients together in a small pan. When quite hot, add the yolk of egg and beat with a rotary egg beater. Add olive oil generously and quickly. The mayonnaise will thicken almost immediately.

· · · · · · · · ·

5.   Mayonnaise

Ingredients

I egg yolk	1/4pt [150ml] olive oil
I saltspoon caster sugar	2 teaspoons vinegar or lemon juice
I saltspoon salt	I saltspoon mustard
I saltspoon cayenne pepper	

Method

Add seasonings to egg yolk, essential to prevent curdling. Beat well, add oil very carefully and slowly at first, so that oil is thoroughly worked in. Later the oil can be more quickly added. Lastly, add the vinegar. (The mayonnaise can be thinned down by adding cream or top of the milk). If the mixture curdles, beat the mixture into another egg yolk, drop by drop. If the mixture is too thick towards the end, add a little vinegar, alternately with the egg yolk. Keep all the ingredients cool and in hot weather wrap the bowl with a wet cloth.

● ● ● ● ● ● ● ● ●

Sandwich Fillings

Sandwich Fillings

1.   Cheese Spread

Ingredients

$^1/_2$lb [225g] grated cheese
$^1/_4$lb [115g] butter
1 egg
salt

$^1/_4$pt [150ml] milk
1 teaspoon made mustard
$^1/_4$ teaspoon cayenne

Method

Melt together the cheese and butter in a saucepan. Beat the egg in a basin, add the milk, mustard, cayenne and one teaspoon salt. To this mixture add the melted cheese and butter. Cook in a double saucepan, stirring all the time, until it is of the consistency of honey.

2.   Cheese and Tomato Spreads

Method for all three spreads

Put the tomatoes into boiling water for a minute, then skin and cut up, place in a pan with the butter.

1. Ingredients

$^1/_2$lb [225g] tomatoes
2oz [50g] breadcrumbs
1 egg, beaten
salt and pepper

1oz [25g] butter
1oz [25g] grated cheese
1 small onion, grated

Add one small grated onion to the pan. When tender mash and add one egg, well beaten and pepper and salt to taste. Stir gently over slow heat until it thickens. Remove from the heat and add 2oz breadcrumbs and 1oz of grated cheese. Put into small pots and cover with melted butter.

2. Ingredients

$^1/_2$lb [225g] tomatoes
1oz [25g] butter
1 egg, beaten

salt and pepper
1oz [25g] grated cheese

When tomatoes are cooked, mash to a pulp, add 1oz [25g] grated cheese, pepper and salt and one beaten egg, stir gently until it thickens. Put into pots.

3. Ingredients

½lb [225g] tomatoes	2 large boiled eggs
1oz [25g] butter	1 tablespoon cornflour
salt and pepper	1 tablespoon milk

When tomatoes are cooked, season with pepper and salt. Mash up two hard boiled eggs with a fork and add to the tomato. Mix 1 tablespoon of cornflour with 1 tablespoon of milk and add to the pan, bring mixture to the boil and cook, stirring all the time until it thickens and the cornflour is done. Sufficient for about one loaf. For sandwiches.

• • • • • • • • •

3.   Potted Chicken

Ingredients

remains of cold chicken	⅓ weight of the chicken, in butter
pepper and salt and a little ground nutmeg	

Method

Remove all skin and bone from the chicken, and mince finely. Season with pepper, salt and mace, add the seasoning by degrees until the right flavour has been obtained. Work in the butter, then press into small jars and seal with melted butter poured on top.

• • • • • • • • •

4.   Mock Crab

Ingredients

3 good sized tomatoes (about ½lb [225g])	1oz [25g] grated cheese and a few
2 eggs	breadcrumbs
pepper and salt	2oz [50g] butter or margarine
milk	1 small onion (chopped)

Method

Skin the tomatoes and stew in the butter with the onion, when cooked add grated cheese. Beat the eggs with just a little milk and about 2 tablespoons of breadcrumbs and seasonings. Stir all in the pan, until it thickens. This mixture is very suitable for sandwiches, but could be used as a tea dish if served on toast. The onion can be omitted and a teaspoon of made mustard substituted.

5.   Fish Spread

Ingredients
I small tin salmon or tuna   4 tablespoons milk
3 eggs ^{1}/4lb [I I 5g] fine breadcrumbs
Ioz [25g] butter   salt and pepper

Method
Beat up the fish. Scramble the eggs with the milk and butter, add salt and pepper to
taste and then beat in the breadcrumbs. Set aside and when cool mix in the fish. A
little tomato sauce or mayonnaise may be added if desired.

• • • • • • • •

6.   Potted Ham

Ingredients
^{1}/2lb [225g] lean cooked ham   mustard
2oz [50g] fat cooked ham   pinch of cayenne
Ioz [25g] butter or fat from the ham

Method
Put the ham through a fine mincer twice, together with the 2oz of fat. Mix well with
a little mustard and the cayenne to taste. Put mixture into small pots and cover with
melted butter.

• • • • • • • •

7.   Relish

Ingredients
Ipt [600ml] red current jelly   2 tablespoons Worcester sauce
I large onion

Method
Melt the jelly in a pan and add the sauce and grated onion. Simmer for a few minutes,
then put into small jars.

• • • • • • • •

8. Neapolitan Sandwiches

Wash and prepare some mushrooms and fry them in butter, chop up finely and allow to cool, use the butter left in the pan to butter slices of thinly cut brown bread. Cut and butter slices of white bread to match. Chop finely and season same chicken or other suitable meat. Add the chopped mushrooms and spread the mixture on top of the brown bread and place a slice of white on top. Press between two boards, cut into pieces and garnish with parsley.

• • • • • • • • •

9. Sandwich Filling

This makes a good filling

Ingredients

¹/₂lb [225g] corned beef   I tablespoon cooked apple
I scrambled egg

Method

Mash corned beef in a pan and heat through. Add scrambled egg and cooked apple.

• • • • • • • • •

10. Sardine Butter

Ingredients

tin of sardines   ¹/₂ teaspoon salt
little butter   ¹/₄ teaspoon pepper

Method

Remove bones from the sardines and add sufficient butter to make a spreading consistency. Add salt and pepper and mix thoroughly. A useful sandwich spread or can be served on hot toast.

• • • • • • • • •

I I. Walnut and Ginger Filling

Method
Shell and chop a few walnuts, and cut up small I or 2 pieces of glace ginger. Stir these together and add a generous supply of whipped cream, spread thickly onto buttered brown bread and form into sandwiches.

• • • • • • • • •

I2. Chocolate and Ginger

Ideal for children's parties

Ingredients
I oz [25g] plain chocolate
I oz [25g] butter

2oz [50g] preserved ginger

Method
Grate the chocolate and cream into the butter, add the chopped ginger and mix well.

• • • • • • • • •

I3. Rum Butter

To be eaten with bread and butter, biscuits or oatcake

Ingredients
I lb [450g] brown sugar (fine Demerara
  or Scotch Moist)
¹/₂lb [225g] butter

¹/₂ to I wine glass of rum
little nutmeg

Method
Melt the butter to oil, mix rum with the sugar, beat together until solid. Before serving, put in fancy dish or bowl and a little grated nutmeg over the top. Will keep for 3 months in a covered dish.

Sauces, Stuffings, and Miscellaneous

1. White Sauce
2. Brown Sauce
3. Apple Sauce
4. Arrowroot Sauce
5. Brandy Sauce
6. Bread Sauce
7. Chaudfroid Sauce
8. Custard Cream Sauce
9. Custard Salad Dressing
10. German Egg Sauce
11. Hard Sauce
12. Hollandaise Sauce
13. Horseradish Sauce
14. Lord Welby's Sauce
15. Italian Sauce
16. Jam Sauce
17. Maître D: Hotel Butter
18. Maître D: Hotel Sauce
19. Mayonnaise
20. Mint Sauce
21. Tomato Sauce
22. Tomato Store Sauce
23. Chestnut Stuffing
24. Sage and Onion Stuffing
25. Veal Forcemeat
26. Boiled Rice for Curries
27. Baking Powder
28. Porridge
29. Batter for Fish
30. Batter for Fritters
31. Yorkshire Pudding

Sauces, Stuffings, and Miscellaneous

Including recipes for sauces etc. used in preceding recipes. The recipes for white and brown sauce given below form the basis of a large variety of sauces of these types. But instructions for the preparation of special sauces are given under special sauces.

1. White Sauce

Ingredients

1oz [25g] butter

1oz [25g] flour

from $^1/_2$ to 1pt [300 to 600ml] milk

flavouring

Method

Melt the butter in a saucepan, stir in the flour. Add the milk, stir until smooth, and boil for a few minutes, stirring the whole time. Add the flavouring as desired. This sauce is the foundation of white vegetable sauce, parsley, caper, onion, anchovy, sweet pudding and egg sauce, etc. To $^1/_2$pt white sauce add: White vegetable sauce, salt and pepper to taste. Parsley sauce, 2 teaspoons chopped parsley and salt and pepper to taste. Caper sauce, 1 teaspoon capers, 1 teaspoon vinegar from the capers and salt and pepper. Onion sauce, 2 large onions chopped up and boiled until tender with salt and pepper to taste. Anchovy sauce, salt and pepper and anchovy essence to taste. Sweet pudding sauce, 1oz sugar and a few drops flavouring essence. Egg sauce for fish, 1 hard boiled egg, chopped, salt and pepper.

2. Brown Vegetable Sauce

Ingredients

I onion
piece of turnip, carrot or swede
stick of celery or I small tomato
I teaspoon cornflour
$^1/_2$ to Ipt [300 to 600ml] brown stock
  or water

salt and pepper
sprig of parsley
I $^1/_2$oz [40g] dripping or butter
Ioz [25g] flour

Method

Cut the vegetables into dice, melt the dripping in a strong saucepan, add the vegetables and parsley. Cover with a lid and heat gently for 10 minutes. Remove the lid and stir occasionally for a further 10 minutes. Remove the vegetables with as little fat as possible. Add the flour, heat and stir until a good brown colour. Add $^1/_2$pt stock gradually, stir to a smooth sauce and boil, stirring all the time. Add the salt and pepper and cook for a few minutes. (The sauce may now be used for binding meat together). Add the vegetables and another $^1/_4$pt stock and leave to simmer gently for another 20 minutes. Strain and serve with chops, steaks and other meat dishes requiring a good brown sauce.

Special Sauces

3.   Apple Sauce

Ingredients

1lb [450g] apples   1oz [25g] butter
2 to 3oz [50 to85g] sugar

Method

Peel and cut up the apples and place in a greased fireproof dish. Add sugar and butter. Cover with greased paper and bake in oven Mark 7/425°F/220°C until tender.

. . . .

4.   Arrowroot Sauce

Ingredients

1 dessertspoon of arrowroot or cornflour   1 tablespoon brandy or sherry
1 tablespoon sugar   1/2pt [300ml] milk
a little flavouring

Method

Mix the arrowroot with a little of the milk cold, add the remainder boiling, pour back into the saucepan, with the sugar and boil for 4 minutes, add 1 tablespoon of brandy or sherry, or any flavouring preferred.

. . . .

5.   Brandy Sauce

Ingredients

I teaspoon cornflour

$^1/_4$pt [150ml] milk

I teaspoon sugar

yolk of egg

$^1/_2$ wine glass of brandy

Method

Mix the cornflour with a little of the milk, heat the remainder of the milk, and when boiling, pour it over the cornflour. Boil, keep stirring for 5 minutes and add the sugar, allow to cool slightly, and then mix in the beaten egg yolk and brandy. Stir until the sauce thickens, but do not boil. The sauce is then ready to serve.

•••••••••

6.   Bread Sauce

Ingredients

I small onion

2 cloves

$^1/_2$pt [300ml] milk

pepper and salt

I tablespoon cream (optional)

3oz [85g] fresh breadcrumbs

Ioz [25g] butter or margarine

Method

Peel the onion and push the cloves into it. Simmer gently with the milk and margarine for at least 20 minutes. Remove the onion and pour the milk over the breadcrumbs (add the cream if using). Let it stand to thicken and reheat before serving.

•••••••••

7.   Chaudfroid Sauce

Ingredients

$^1/_2$pt [300ml] white sauce (see recipe)

$^1/_4$pt [150ml] aspic jelly (see recipe)

$^1/_4$pt [150ml] cream

Method

Make the white sauce, add the melted aspic jelly and the cream and stir until cool, but not setting, then use for coating chicken, hard boiled eggs, etc. N.B. $^3/_4$pt of white sauce may be used in place of $^1/_2$pt sauce and $^1/_4$pt cream.

8.   Custard Cream Sauce

Ingredients

3 egg yolks

³/₄pt [450ml] milk

1oz [25g] sugar

flavouring

Method

Beat the egg yolks and add the milk, hot but not boiling. Beat together, turn into a jug and stand in a saucepan of water, or use a double saucepan. Place over a burner and stir until the mixture thickens, using only a small flame to avoid curdling the custard. Add the sugar and flavouring.

• • • • • • • • •

9.   Custard Salad Dressing

Ingredients

¹/₄pt [150ml] milk

1 small teaspoon custard powder

vinegar

cayenne

sugar

mustard

salt

Method

Mix the custard powder with a little of the milk cold, add the remainder boiling, pour back into the saucepan and boil. When cold, add vinegar, sugar, mustard, etc., to taste.

• • • • • • • • •

10.   German Egg Sauce

Ingredients

1 egg

1 dessertspoon sugar

¹/₄pt [150ml] sherry

1 strip lemon peel

Method

Put all into a basin, the sherry being slightly warmed. Place the basin over a pan of hot water, whisk briskly for 10 minutes or until the sauce has a froth. (Take care it does not get too hot, or it will curdle). Serve at once.

11. Hard Sauce

Ingredients

¹/4lb [115g] fresh butter

¹/4lb [115g] sugar

1 tablespoon sherry or brandy

2oz [50g] ground almonds

Method

Beat the butter and sugar to a cream, add brandy or sherry and the ground almonds. Serve piled up on a dish. The almonds may be omitted.

• • • • • • • • •

12. Hollandaise Sauce

Ingredients

¹/2pt [300ml] white sauce (hot)

salt and pepper

1 to 4 yolks of eggs

a little milk or stock

juice of small lemon

1 to 2oz [25 to 50g] butter

Method

Flavour the half pint of freshly made white sauce, with the salt and pepper, add the yolks or eggs and beat together over a low flame until cooked and thick. Thin to the consistency required with the milk or stock and lemon juice. Take from the hotplate and gradually add the butter, divided into small pieces. Pass through a fine strainer.

• • • • • • • • •

13. Horseradish Sauce

Ingredients

4 tablespoons grated horseradish

1 teaspoon sugar

1 teaspoon salt

¹/2 teaspoon pepper

2 teaspoons made mustard

vinegar

3 tablespoons cream (if liked)

Method

Mix all the ingredients together and serve. If required hot, heat in a double pan or in a pan of water. This sauce may be kept in a corked bottle for some time.

14.   Lord Welby's Sauce

A delicious substitute for horseradish sauce

Ingredients

2 tablespoons of cream
1 tablespoon mustard
1 tablespoon grated parsnip

little salt
1 tablespoon vinegar

Method

Mix all the ingredients together and serve in a sauceboat. The parsnip being sweet requires no sugar. (The story of this recipe is, that Lord Welby used to dine frequently at Christ Church College and on one occasion, there was no horseradish sauce. The cook made a substitute sauce with parsnip and Lord Welby said that it was the best horseradish sauce he had ever tasted).

• • • • • • • • •

15.   Italian Sauce

Ingredients

1 small onion, chopped
1oz [25g] butter
3 or 4 mushrooms chopped
¹/₂pt [300ml] gravy
¹/₄pt [150ml] white wine (optional)

2 truffles chopped (optional)
1 teaspoon chopped parsley
pepper
cayenne

Method

Fry the onions and mushrooms lightly in the butter, add the gravy and (wine if used) boil well. Add the truffles, parsley, pepper and cayenne, and serve.

• • • • • • • • •

16.   Jam Sauce

Ingredients

2 tablespoons jam
2 tablespoons water

1 teaspoon lemon juice

Method

Place the ingredients together in a saucepan and bring to the boil. Boil a few minutes, take off heat, stand for a few minutes and serve.

17.   Maître D'Hotel Butter

Ingredients

2oz [50g] butter

2 dessertspoons parsley

a few drops lemon juice

salt and pepper

Method

Pick the parsley carefully, chop finely and mix thoroughly with the butter, seasoning and lemon juice. Serve in pats with grills, fish etc.

•••••••••

18.   Maître D'Hotel Sauce

Ingredients

2oz [50g] butter

salt and pepper

2 teaspoons chopped parsley

lemon juice

Method

Melt the butter, stir in the parsley, seasoning and a few drops of lemon juice. Serve over fish, cutlets etc., or in a tureen.

•••••••••

19.   Mayonnaise

Ingredients

1 yolk of egg, raw

$^1/_4$ to $^1/_2$pt [150 to 300ml] salad oil

cream

vinegar

lemon juice

mustard (made)

salt, sugar and pepper

cayenne

Method

Put the yolk into a basin, add the salad oil drop by drop, stirring briskly the whole time. If the oil is added carefully, one yolk of egg will thicken $^1/_2$pt of oil. This mixture will keep for a time. To make mayonnaise, take as much as is required of the egg and oil mixture, add to it vinegar, cream, mustard etc., until the required taste is obtained.

•••••••••

20. Mint Sauce

Ingredients

2 tablespoons finely chopped mint
3 tablespoons brown sugar

a little boiling water
vinegar

Method

Place the chopped mint in a sauceboat, add sugar, just cover with boiling water. When cold, add as much vinegar as liked.

• • • • • • • •

21. Tomato Sauce

Ingredients

2oz [50g] butter
1/2 onion
1oz [25g] flour
1/2pt [300ml] stock or water
a few drops of cochineal

1/2 carrot
3/4lb [350g] tomatoes or half a tin
pepper
1/2 teaspoon salt

Method

Cut up the carrot and onion and fry them in the butter for ten minutes. Add the flour, stock, seasoning and tomatoes, bring to the boil, simmer slowly for 30 minutes. Pass through a hairsieve, rubbing as much pulp as possible. Reheat and serve. If necessary a few drops of cochineal may be added to improve the colour.

• • • • • • • •

22. Tomato Store Sauce

Ingredients

3lb [1.35kg] red tomatoes
1 small onion
1 clove
10 peppercorns

1 dessertspoon salt
1/2pt [300ml] vinegar
3oz [85g] sugar
1 bay leaf

Method

Cut the tomatoes in half. Chop the onion, place all the ingredients except the sugar in a pan and simmer for 1 hour. Pass through a sieve, return to the saucepan and boil hard to reduce to a thin cream. Add the sugar, pour the sauce into bottles, when cold, cork tightly and store.

Stuffings

23. Chestnut Stuffing for Turkey

Ingredients

2lb [900g] chestnuts
¹/₂pt [300ml] milk or stock
1 to 2oz [25 to 50g] butter

salt and pepper
¹/₄ teaspoon sugar

Method

Cut off the tops from the chestnuts, roast for 20 minutes. Remove outer and inner skins, put the chestnuts in a pan with the stock. Simmer gently until tender. Rub through a sieve, add butter, salt, pepper and sugar. Use for stuffing breast of Turkey.

24. Sage and Onion Stuffing

Ingredients

1lb [450g] onions
1 teaspoon crushed sage

¹/₄lb [115g] breadcrumbs
salt and pepper

Method

Cut the onions into quarters, drop into boiling water containing a little salt. Parboil for 15 minutes, drain, chop, add sage, salt, pepper and breadcrumbs. Use for stuffing, pork, ducks, geese, etc.

25. Veal Forcemeat

Ingredients

1/4lb [115g] breadcrumbs
2oz [50g] chopped suet
1 tablespoon parsley
1 teaspoon dried herbs

a little grated lemon rind
egg or milk for mixing
salt and pepper

Method
Make a mixture of all the ingredients, using sufficient beaten egg or milk to moisten it. Use for stuffing, veal, fowl etc. The forcemeat may also be formed into small balls, rolled in flour and fried and used as a garnish for stews.

• • • • • • • •

26. Boiled Rice for Curries

Method
Patna rice will be found to be the best for curries. It must be washed thoroughly and thrown into plenty of boiling water, containing 1 teaspoon salt and a few drops of lemon juice to each quart of water. Boil for 15 to 20 minutes or until the grains will break between the thumb and finger. Drain on a wire sieve, rinse in cold water, dry and reheat, keeping the grains quite separate. Dish as a vegetable.

• • • • • • • •

27. Home Made Baking Powder

Method

2oz [50g] cream of tartar
1oz [25g] bicarbonate soda

3oz [85g] ground rice

Method
Mix the ingredients together and pass them through a fine sieve 4 or 5 times. Keep in a tin with a good fitting lid, in a dry place. (This baking powder is of the correct strength to use in the proportions given for recipes in this book.)

• • • • • • • •

28. Porridge – The Old Fashioned Way

Ingredients

2pt [1.2 litre] water
¹/₂lb [225g] rolled oats or 6oz [175g]
    coarse oatmeal

¹/₂ to 1 teaspoon salt

Method

Boil the water, and when boiling, sprinkle in the oats, stirring all the time. Cook gently, for 2 hours stirring frequently. If a double saucepan is used, the porridge will only need stirring very occasionally. Porridge can be made overnight and heated up for breakfast.

•••••••••

29. Batter for Fish

Ingredients

¹/₄lb [115g] flour
1 egg

¹/₄pt [150ml] milk or water
salt

Method

Break the egg into a well made in the flour, add the milk slowly, gradually stirring in the flour. Beat until smooth and allow to stand for 1 hour before using.

•••••••••

30. Batter for Fritters

Ingredients

¹/₄lb [115g] flour
¹/₄pt [150ml] warm water
2 teaspoons salad oil

1 white of egg
pinch of salt

Method

Make a batter with the flour, salt and salad oil and water. Allow to stand for 1 hour. Just before using the batter, fold in the white of egg, beaten stiffly.

•••••••••

31.   Yorkshire Pudding

The typical Yorkshire pudding is generally made with milk and water, so as to obtain lightness and crispness. For a crisp pudding it is essential there is no fat in the mixture. The other essentials for a good pudding are very hot fat and not too much of it and a good hot oven. Traditionally, Yorkshire pudding should be eaten with thick gravy, before the main meat course. The old method of cooking was to place the pudding in the roasting tin underneath the joint which was being roasted on a spit. The juices would then drip down on to the cooking pudding.

Ingredients
I egg
I teaspoon salt
^{1}/4pt [150ml] water

^{1}/4lb [115g] flour
^{1}/4pt [150ml] milk

Method
Break the egg into the flour and salt, previously mixed in a basin. Add enough liquid to make a beating consistency, beat well and leave to stand for half an hour. Heat oven to Mark 8/450°F/230°C for small puddings. Use 2^1/2" by 1" bun tray, and put a knob of fat in each tin. Place the tray in the oven until fat is smoking hot. In the meantime, add the rest of the liquid to make a batter. Take the tray from the oven and using a long handled spoon, put 2 tablespoons into each tin. Bake for 15 to 20 minutes. Serve with rich onion gravy.

• • • • • • • • •

Invalid Recipes

1. Barley Water
2. Apple Water
3. Lemonade
4. Beef Tea Raw
5. Beef Tea Cooked
6. Nourishing Beef Tea
7. Soups for Invalids
8. Egg Jelly
9. Savoury Custard
10. Egg Nog
11. Strengthening Tonic
12. Steamed Fillet Sole or other White Fish
13. Stewed Eel
14. Coddled Egg
15. Invalid Poached Egg
16. Coffee and Egg Nog
17. Tea or Cocoa Egg Nog
18. Steamed Chop
19. Chicken
20. Chicken Quenelles
21. Sweetbread
22. Calf's Foot Jelly

Sweets

23. Milk Jelly
24. Invalid Pudding
25. Light Baked Pudding
26. Soothing Syrup
27. Bread and Milk

Invalid Recipes

1.   Barley Water

Ingredients

2 to 4oz [50 to 115g] barley, according
   to thickness desired
$^1/_2$ to 1oz [15 to 25g] sugar

1 quart [1.2 litre] water
1 lemon

Method

Wash the barley, place in a saucepan with the water and simmer gently for 1 hour or more. If the lemon is used, strain, add sugar and lemon juice if liked (note barley may be used a second time if the cooking has not been for much longer than 1 hour).

2.   Apple Water

Ingredients

$^1/_2$lb [225g] apples
sugar to taste

$^1/_2$ to 1pt [300 to 600ml] water
1 lemon

Method

Wash and wipe the apples, chop them without first peeling, place them in a jug and cover with boiling water. Add sugar and rind and juice of a lemon, if liked. Stir and leave to cool. Strain and serve. (The peelings only of apples may be used for apple water.)

3.   Lemonade

Ingredients

1 lemon $1/2$pt [300ml] boiling water

sugar to taste

Method

Well wash the lemon, grate or peel thinly the rind off the lemon and soak in some of the boiling water. Dissolve the sugar in the remainder of the water. Add the juice of the lemon to the sugar and water, and the water strained from the lemon rind. Serve when quite cold. To make effervescing, add $1/2$ teaspoon of bicarbonate soda to each glass of lemonade. Stir well and serve at once.

• • • • • • • • •

4.   Beef Tea (Raw)

Ingredients

$1/2$lb [225g] gravy beef   pinch of salt

$1/2$pt [300ml] cold water

Method

Scrape the beef from the skin with a sharp knife and remove all fat, add salt and cover with cold water. Leave to stand for 2 to 3 hours. Stir and strain and serve in a red glass.

• • • • • • • • •

5.   Beef Tea (Cooked)

Method

Prepare as for beef tea raw, but cook very slowly for 1 hour or longer, instead of soaking. Use a double saucepan. Serve in a cup, skimming the fat off with soft paper.

• • • • • • • • •

6.   Nourishing Beef Tea

Ingredients
¹/₄pt [150ml] made beef tea

yolk of an egg

1 teaspoon sago

1 to 2 tablespoons cream

Method
Soak the sago in a ¹/₄pt water for 30 minutes. Cook in a double saucepan and when clear add ¹/₄pt of beef tea. Heat without boiling, then remove from heat and add the well beaten yolk of egg and the cream. Serve at once.

• • • • • • • • •

7.   Soups for Invalids

Soups made from meat e.g. mutton broth, chicken broth, kidney soup, also barley cream soup and soup made from good bone stock, are all suitable for invalids. They must be quite free from grease and not too highly flavoured. Wine may be added to the soup, if allowed by the doctor. Vegetables are not too easily digested and should be used very sparingly in flavouring meat soups. Barley, rice and semolina or vermicelli can be used for thickening.

• • • • • • • • •

8.   Egg Jelly

Ingredients
¹/₂oz [15g] gelatine

6oz [175g] lump sugar

water

1 lemon or 2 oranges

1 egg

Method
Put gelatine in a pan with rind of lemon (or oranges) and sugar and well beaten egg. Make up fruit juice to 1pt with water, and add. bring just to the boil, stirring well all the time and strain. Put in a rinsed mould.

• • • • • • • • •

9.   Savoury Custard

Ingredients

I egg	salt and pepper
¹/₄pt [150ml] beef tea	sprig of parsley

Method

Grease a small mould or shallow jar lightly with butter. Beat the egg, pour the beef tea over the egg, stirring all the time, season to taste. Pour into the prepared mould, cover with greased paper and tie down. Place an inverted saucer or pie dish in the bottom of a pan with boiling water. Stand the custard on top. The water should come halfway up the jar. Steam gently for 15 to 20 minutes, until custard is set. Take it out, stand for 1 minute, then turn out carefully onto a dainty plate and garnish. May be served hot or cold.

· · · · · · · · ·

10.   Egg Nog

Ingredients

I egg	¹/₂pt [300 ml] milk
salt and sugar to taste	I tablespoon brandy

Method

Beat the egg well and whisk in the milk, which may be warm or cold. Add sugar and salt to taste and the brandy. If the white of egg only be used, a tablespoon of cream can be added with the milk.

· · · · · · · · ·

11.   Strengthening Tonic

Ingredients

2 new laid eggs	¹/₄pt [150ml] rum
2 large lemons	¹/₂pt [300ml] milk
¹/₄lb [115g] sugar	

Method

Put the eggs in a basin in their shells, squeeze the juice of the lemons over the eggs, placing the pulp on top. Cover up and keep airtight for 5 days until the shells are nearly dissolved. Then mix together. Strain and add sugar, milk and rum. Mix well and put into clean dry bottles. Cork securely, label and date.

Dose: One wine glass mixed with a little warm water taken, fasting, first thing in the morning.

·····
Fish
·····

The most suitable methods of cooking fish for invalids, are steaming and baking. Grilling may also be allowed, but boiling and frying are unsuitable.

·········

12. Steamed Fillet of Sole, or other White Fish

Method
Butter a soup plate, place the fillet either flat or rolled up on the plate and sprinkle lightly with salt and a few drops of lemon juice. Cover with another plate and place over a pan of boiling water. Cook for 20 to 30 minutes, according to the thickness of the fish. Serve with the creamy liquid which will run from the fish, if allowed. A little sauce may be served with the fish. As a variation, the fish, when cooked, may be broken up with a fork and mixed with the liquid on the soup plate and then served on hot buttered toast or creamed potatoes.

·········

13.   Stewed Eel

Ingredients
I eel   ¹/₂pt [300ml] white or brown sauce

Method
Wash the eel and cut into pieces, place in a double saucepan, cover with water and cook for about 20 to 30 minutes. Pour off the water and add the sauce to the eel. Cook for about 45 minutes, until quite tender. Serve with the sauce and small pieces of toast.

·········

Egg Dishes

14. Coddled Egg (1)

Method

Place an egg in a pan of boiling water, cover with a lid and remove from the burner. Leave to stand in a warm place for 10 minutes.

Coddled Egg (2)

Place an egg in a pan of cold water, bring the water to the boil, remove from the burner, and leave the egg in the hot water for a few minutes.

15. Invalid Poached Egg

Method

Pour about 2 tablespoons of milk into a small saucepan and into this, break an egg. Warm gently until the egg has just set. Turn out carefully on to a round of buttered toast.

16. Coffee and Egg Nog

This is good to serve in cases of exhaustion, as it is stimulating, nourishing and easy to digest.

Ingredients

1 egg   sugar
cup of hot coffee and milk

Method

Beat the egg well and whisk in the coffee and milk. Add sugar to taste.

17. Tea or Cocoa Egg Nog

Make as for coffee nog, substituting freshly made tea or cocoa in place of coffee.

• • • • • • • • •

18. Steamed Chop

Ingredients

1 chop $^1/_2$oz [15g] rice

Method

Place the chop in a double saucepan with a dessertspoon of water. Cook for 30 to 40 minutes, according to size. Place the rice in rapidly boiling salted water and cook until tender. Strain and place on a hot dish. Serve the chop on the rice with any gravy that has run out of it. If preferred, creamed potatoes may be used in place of the rice.

• • • • • • • • •

19. Chicken

Method

The breast of chicken is usually given to an invalid. It may be taken from a steamed, boiled, or baked chicken or may be cooked separately. The legs and carcass can then be used for chicken broth. To cook the breast only, steam between 2 plates, as for fillet of sole (recipe given). If allowed, serve with white sauce or bread sauce.

• • • • • • • • •

20. Chicken Quenelles

Ingredients

$^1/_4$lb [115g] breast of chicken 'uncooked'   1 egg
1oz [25g] breadcrumbs   salt and pepper
a little stock or milk

Method

Mince the chicken and pound with the beaten egg. Add the breadcrumbs, salt and pepper and just sufficient stock or milk to moisten. The mixture must not be too moist. Form into egg shapes with 2 dessertspoons and place in a buttered omelette pan. Pour hot water round the quenelles. Cover with buttered paper and cook slowly for 20 minutes, serve with gravy. Beef or veal may be used in place of the chicken.

21. Sweetbread

Ingredients

1 lambs sweetbread	1/2oz [15g] butter
milk	1/2oz [15g] flour
salt and pepper	toast
sprig of fresh parsley	

Method

Wash and soak the sweetbread in salted water for 1 or 2 hours. Place it in a pan and cover with cold water. Bring slowly to the boil. Drain off the water and dip the sweetbread into cold water to cool. Remove all fat and skin. Cover with milk and then flavour with pepper and salt and parsley. Simmer gently on the hotplate in a double saucepan or cook in a casserole in the oven for one hour and 15 minutes, with the Regulo at Mark 1/2. Melt the butter in a saucepan. Add the flour and cook together for 1 minute, then add the milk from the sweetbread, stir smoothly and bring to the boil to make a sauce. Pour the sauce over the sweetbread and serve with sippets of toast. If the sauce is too rich, serve the sweetbread on a round of toast with a little of the milk in which it was cooked.

● ● ● ● ● ● ● ● ●

22. Calf's Foot Jelly or Cowheel Jelly

Ingredients

2 calf's feet or cow heel	rind of 3 lemons
2 quarts [2.4 litres] water	6oz [175g] sugar
3/4 pt [450ml] lemon juice and white wine mixed	whites and shells of 2 eggs

Method

Divide the feet into pieces. Place them in a saucepan. Cover with cold water and bring to the boil. Pour off this water and throw it away. Add the 2 quarts of water to the feet, cover and simmer gently for 5 or 6 hours. Strain and leave until quite cold, when the liquid will have set in a jelly. Carefully remove all fat and place the jelly in a large saucepan with the lemon rind, juice, wine and sugar and washed and crushed shells of the eggs. Partly whisk the whites of the eggs and then add to the other ingredients. Whisk steadily bringing all to the boil. Leave to boil without whisking for 3 to 5 minutes, then allow to stand for 10 minutes. Pour carefully through a jelly bag, first placing a cupful of the scum from the top of the jelly into the bag to act as a filter. Turn into a jelly mould and leave to set.

Sweets

Milk puddings, custards, jellies, steamed or lightly baked puddings, stewed fruit and cream or custard would all be suitable for invalids. A pudding rich in egg should not follow a first course containing egg. A milk diet may include milk jellies, the only addition to the milk being gelatine and a little sugar and flavouring.

23. Milk Jelly

Ingredients

1/2pt [300ml] milk	1 tablespoon water
strip of lemon rind	1/2oz [15g] gelatine
1/2oz [15g] sugar	1 tablespoon cream

Method

Simmer the lemon rind in the milk for 20 minutes, add the sugar. Remove the lemon rind and leave the milk to cool. Dissolve the gelatine in the water, mix the milk and gelatine when both are cool. If the milk is too cool the gelatine may set in lumps, but if too hot, the milk may curdle. Add the cream, stir and turn into a mould to set. Note: The gelatine may be dissolved in the milk, but this frequently results in the curdling of the milk. It is better, therefore, to dissolve the gelatine in water and add the cream.

24. Invalid Pudding

Ingredients

^{1}/2oz [15g] ground rice
^{1}/2oz [15g] caster sugar
^{1}/4 lemon rind, grated

^{1}/2pt [300ml] milk
1 egg
pinch of salt

Method

Mix the ground rice with 1 tablespoon of milk, add it to the remainder of the milk, boiling, also the sugar, lemon rind and a pinch of salt. Pour back into the saucepan and boil for 3 to 4 minutes. Beat the yolk and the white of the egg separately, add the yolk to the milk etc., then the white, which must be lightly stirred in. Pour into a buttered pie dish and bake for half hour at Gas Mark 4/350°F/180°C. Serve hot or cold.

• • • • • • • • •

25. Light Baked Pudding

Ingredients

^{1}/2pt [300ml] milk
^{1}/4pt [150ml] breadcrumbs
grated lemon or orange rind

2 eggs
1oz [25g] butter
1oz [25g] caster sugar

Method

Pour the milk over the breadcrumbs and leave to soak for 30 minutes. Separate the yolks from the whites of the eggs. Beat the yolks into the milk and crumbs. Add the sugar rind and whites of eggs stiffly whipped. Turn into a well greased pie dish, cover with little dabs of butter. Bake for 30 minutes at Gas Mark 5/375°F/190°C. Flaked rice or similar preparations may be used in place of breadcrumbs.

• • • • • • • • •

26. Soothing Syrup

For hoarseness, sore throats etc.

Ingredients

2 tablespoon honey
I dessertspoon of vinegar
I teaspoon sugar

juice of I lemon
I dessertspoon of glycerine
$1/4$pt [150ml] hot water

Method

Mix all together in a glass and sip hot or cold. The proportions may be varied to taste and if preferred, the water can be omitted.

• • • • • • • • •

27. Bread and Milk

This was my children's supper dish and also given to adults when 'off colour'.

Ingredients

slice of bread
$1/2$pt [300ml] milk

pinch of salt
sugar if liked

Method

There are three methods in common use. The following method is usually advised for invalids. Remove the crust and cut the bread in to squares and add it to the boiling milk. Cook for about I minute, add a pinch of salt and serve with sugar if liked. Some people prefer the bread placed in the cold milk and the bread and milk then heated together. This may be done in a double saucepan. Salt and sugar can be added as liked. The third method is to place the cut bread in a bowl, and add boiling milk, stir and add salt and sugar if liked.

• • • • • • • • •

Cheese, Egg and Vegetarian Dishes

1. Bean Cutlets
2. Bread Steaks
3. Cheese Pudding
4. Curried Eggs
5. Macaroni Savoury
6. Vegetable Pie

Cheese, Egg and Vegetarian Dishes

1. Bean Cutlets

Ingredients

½lb [225g] beans (butter or haricot)
1½oz [40g] butter
1 large tomato
1oz [25g] flour
½oz [15g] curry powder
Maître d'Hotel butter

¼pt [150ml] vegetable stock or
   water
salt and pepper
2oz [50g] chopped raisins
2oz [50g] breadcrumbs

Method

Soak overnight, then boil the beans and pass them through a sieve. Heat the butter in a frying pan or saucepan and fry the sliced tomato. Add the flour and curry powder, stir and fry for a few minutes. Add the water or stock, stir and boil. Add the salt, pepper, sieved beans, raisins and breadcrumbs and mix well together. Turn onto a floured plate and allow to cool. Cut into 2 pieces and shape into cutlets. Place on cake tray, brush over with egg and bake in the oven for 15 minutes Mark 7/425°F/220°C. Alternatively, brush with egg and dip in crumbs, press the crumbs on with a knife and fry in hot fat. Serve with Maître d'Hotel butter (see sauces).

• • • • • • • • •

2.   Bread Steaks

Ingredients

6 rounds of bread
1 teaspoon chopped parsley
1 egg
salt and pepper

3oz [85g] breadcrumbs
a little milk
a little fat or butter for frying
1/2 teaspoon sweet herbs

Method

Remove the crusts from the bread and divide into neat pieces, moisten with the milk; beat up the egg and add it to the salt, pepper, sweet herbs and parsley. Dip the pieces of bread in this, then roll them in breadcrumbs, fry a nice brown in hot butter or fat. Dish in a ring with fried onions, tomatoes or mushrooms in centre.

• • • • • • • • •

3.   Cheese Pudding

Ingredients

some thin slices of bread and butter
6oz [175g] grated cheese
pepper and salt

3 eggs
1pt [600ml] milk

Method

Butter a pie dish, arrange in it alternate layers of bread and butter and grated cheese, with pepper and salt. Beat up the eggs, add them to the milk, pour over the bread and butter etc. Allow to stand for half an hour. Bake for 45 minutes Mark 3/325°F160°C.

• • • • • • • • •

4.   Curried Eggs

Ingredients

4 hard boiled eggs
1oz [25g] butter
¹/₂oz [15g] curry powder
¹/₂oz [15g] flour
¹/₂ small apple and 1 onion

¹/₂pt [300ml] stock or water
few drops lemon juice
1 teaspoon chutney
2oz [50g] rice
salt, parsley to garnish

Method

Melt the butter in a small saucepan. In it brown the thinly sliced onion, stir in the curry powder, flour, stock and chopped apple; simmer gently for 30 minutes. Cut 3 of the hard boiled eggs in halves. To the curry sauce add salt, lemon juice and chutney and reheat the eggs in the sauce. Pour into a dish, cut up the remaining egg into small pieces and use as a garnish together with the parsley and serve with a border of cooked rice.

· · · · · · · · ·

5.   Macaroni Savoury

Ingredients

¹/₂lb [225g] best macaroni
¹/₂pt [300ml] stock (well seasoned)
2 tomatoes

1oz [25g] butter
¹/₂oz [15g] flour
2oz [50g] cheese

Method

Boil the macaroni in plenty of water with a little salt until soft, drain it. Boil the tomato (cut up) in the stock until quite soft, strain. Melt the butter, stir in the flour, add stock and boil. Dish the macaroni in layers, with grated cheese between each layer and a little of the sauce. When all the macaroni is dished, pour the remainder of the sauce over it.

· · · · · · · · ·

6.   Vegetable Pie

Ingredients

1lb [450g] mashed potatoes
$^1/_4$lb [115g] each of cooked turnips,
   carrots, haricot beans

$^1/_2$lb [225g] tomatoes
$^1/_4$pt [150ml] brown sauce or gravy
1oz [25g] butter

Method

Grease a pie dish and arrange the sliced turnip, carrot, tomatoes and haricot beans in layers. Pour over $^1/_4$pt well seasoned brown sauce or gravy. Cover with mashed potatoes and put on the butter, broken into small pieces. Bake for 20 minutes in preheated oven Mark 7/425°F/220°C.

Home Made Sweets

1. Almond Truffles
2. Caramel Creams
3. Cherry Cups
4. Chocolate Fudge
5. Coconut Ice
6. Coconut Nuggets
7. Coffee Walnut Creams
8. Honeycomb Toffee
9. Marshmallows
10. Peppermint Creams
11. Rum Truffles
12. Toffee Brazils
13. Swiss Toffee

Home Made Sweets

Really good confectionery is very expensive these days, so, why not make your own? When in doubt over what to give as presents, something home-made is especially welcome. A box of fudge, coconut ice, toffee appeals to all age groups.

1. Almond Truffles

Ingredients

1oz [25g] flaked almonds
2oz [50g] ground almonds
2oz [50g] sponge cake crumbs
2 drops of almond essence

2 tablespoons apricot jam
1oz [25g] icing sugar
2oz [50g] chocolate

Method

Brown the flaked almonds by putting under the grill, or placing in a slow oven until light brown, mix ground almonds, cake crumbs and sieved icing sugar. Melt the chocolate in a small bowl over a pan of hot water. Stir the chocolate in the ground almond mixture with the almond essence and mix well. Roll into small balls. Heat apricot jam gently, dip each truffle into the jam to coat and roll in browned flaked almonds. Makes 12 truffles.

2.   Caramel Creams

Ingredients

6oz [175g] granulated sugar
1/4 teaspoon salt
8 tablespoons syrup
1 teaspoon vanilla essence

2oz [50g] butter
1 small can carnation milk
(5 1/2floz [175ml])

Method

Put all ingredients except the vanilla into a saucepan. Stir over low heat until sugar is dissolved. Boil, stirring until temperature of 245°F is reached. Add vanilla, pour into an oiled 7" square tin. When set, cut into squares and wrap in waxed paper.

• • • • • • • • •

3.   Cherry Cups

Ingredients

18 maraschino cherries

For Almond Paste

1/4lb [115g] ground almonds
1/4lb [115g] icing sugar
1 egg yolk
1 teaspoon lemon juice

2 drops almond essence
pink colouring
a little chocolate (optional)

Method

Drain the maraschino cherries from their syrup. Mix the ground almonds and sieved icing sugar in a small bowl. Add the yolk, lemon juice, almond essence and enough pink colouring to make the mixture a pale pink. Mix ingredients evenly to a smooth stiff paste. Divide the almond paste into 18 small pieces. Press each piece of almond paste round a cherry, leaving part of the cherry showing at the top. If liked, dip the base of each cherry cup in a little melted chocolate. Makes 18 sweets.

• • • • • • • • •

4. Chocolate Fudge

Ingredients

¹/₂lb [225g] plain chocolate
I standard egg
I lb [450g] icing sugar (sieved)

I oz [25g] margarine
I small tin condensed milk
I teaspoon coffee essence or
   ¹/₂ teaspoon vanilla essence

Method

Lightly oil a 7" square shallow tin, melt the chocolate in a bowl over a pan of hot water. Add the margarine and the egg, stir until well blended, add remaining ingredients and beat until the mixture begins to thicken. Pour mixture into the tin and mark into I" squares. Leave in a cool place until set. Makes about I lb 12oz.

• • • • • • • • •

5. Coconut Ice

A very simple recipe which requires no cooking.

Ingredients

I large tin condensed milk (size
   equivalent to I ⁵/₈pt [975ml] milk)
³/₄lb [350g icing sugar

³/₄lb [350g] desiccated coconut
pink edible food colouring

Method

Mix the condensed milk with the icing sugar. Stir in the coconut to make a very stiff mixture; divide in half. Colour half the mixture pale pink. Shape each colour into two equal sized bars and press pink and white halves firmly together. Dust a baking sheet or plate with icing sugar and leave the coconut ice on this until firm and set.

• • • • • • • • •

6.   Coconut Nuggets

Ingredients

2 standard egg whites

1/4lb [115g] caster sugar

4 to 5oz [115 to 140g] coconut

pink colouring

Method

Prepare a slow oven Gas Mark 3/325°F/170°C. Place a sheet of rice paper on a baking tray. Place the egg whites in a bowl and whisk until stiff. Fold in the caster sugar and coconut with a metal spoon until evenly mixed. Place half the mixture in small teaspoonfuls on the rice paper. Colour the remaining mixture a pale pink and then continue to spoon on the rice paper. Cook in the oven for 15 minutes. Makes 18 nuggets.

• • • • • • • • •

7.   Coffee Walnut Creams

N.B. These sweets will not keep for long.

Ingredients

icing sugar

coffee essence

white of egg

shelled walnuts

Method

Crush with a rolling pin any lumps in the icing sugar. Add sufficient coffee essence and white of egg to colour, flavour and make the sugar cling together whilst working in the mixture well together by hand. Turn on to a slab sprinkled with icing sugar and knead until quite smooth. Divide and shape into small balls. Press half a walnut onto each ball. If the walnuts will not stick, brush the ball with white of egg. Leave to set.

• • • • • • • • •

8.   Honeycomb Toffee

Makes about 2lb [900g]

Ingredients

1½lb [675g] granulated sugar
½ level teaspoon cream of tartar
6oz [175g] hazelnuts or peanuts (chopped)

2oz [50g] margarine
1 level teaspoon bicarbonate soda
½pt [300ml] water

Method

Grease a shallow tin about 7" by 11", put ½pt water in a pan with the sugar and cream of tartar. Stir over a gentle heat until mixture is completely dissolved, then bring to the boil and cook slowly until the mixture is light brown. When a little is dropped into cold water it should set hard and brittle. Stir in the margarine, chopped nuts and bicarbonate of soda. Pour into greased tin. Leave until cold and set. Break up into pieces.

• • • • • • • • •

9.   Marshmallows

Ingredients

1oz [25g] gelatine
1pt [600ml] water
1lb [450g] sugar
¼ teaspoon cream of tartar

pinch of salt
1 teaspoon vanilla essence
little mixed icing sugar and
    cornflower for coating

Method

Soak the gelatine in ½pt of cold water. Dissolve sugar in ½pt of boiling water and boil with cream of tartar to soft ball stage (a little in cold water forms a ball, which loses its shape when taken from the water). Add essence and salt to gelatine and pour boiling syrup on slowly. Whisk until thick and white. Pour into greased tin and the following day cut into squares and roll in the mixed icing sugar and cornflour.

• • • • • • • • •

10. Peppermint Creams

Ingredients
1lb [450g] sieved icing sugar
about 1 tablespoon of sweetened
   condensed milk

few drops of oil of peppermint

Method
Mix the sugar and milk together to a pliable dough. Knead well, add a few drops of oil of peppermint and knead to mix. Roll out on a board sprinkled with icing sugar and cut into small rounds. Alternatively, roll small balls in the hand, and then flatten them on the sugared board. Set aside until firm.

· · · · · · · · ·

11. Rum Truffles

Ingredients
6oz [175g] plain chocolate
1oz [25g] butter
1 tablespoon rum
chocolate vermicelli or powder

2 egg yolks
1 dessertspoon thick cream
6 to 8oz [175 to 225g] icing sugar

Method
Melt the chocolate in a basin over hot water, without allowing it to get too hot. Remove from the heat, add the yolks, butter cream and rum. Beat well until smooth then add enough of the sifted icing sugar gradually until the mixture just holds together. Form into small balls between two teaspoons, then roll these in chocolate vermicelli or drinking chocolate powder.

· · · · · · · · ·

12. Toffee Brazils

Ingredients
1lb [450g] granulated sugar
2 level teaspoons glucose

1/4pt [150ml] water
1/2lb [225g] shelled walnuts

Method
Dissolve sugar in a pan with glucose and 1/4pt water. Bring to the boil. Boil for 8 minutes. Drop nuts into the toffee, a few at a time. Spoon coated nuts one by one onto a greased baking sheet.

• • • • • • • • •

13. Swiss Toffee

Ingredients
2oz [50g] butter
1lb [450g] caster sugar
1 tablespoon golden syrup

small tin condensed milk
2 teaspoons vanilla essence

Method
Rinse out a strong pan with cold water. Leave a little water in and add the butter, syrup and sugar. When melted, add the condensed milk and boil for 20 minutes. Remove from the heat and add the vanilla essence. Stir well and pour in a greased tin. This toffee may also be made without the vanilla essence or with chopped walnuts added in place of the vanilla.